COLLECTED POEMS

KEVIN
CROSSLEY-HOLLAND

Collected Poems

2025

Published by Arc Publications,
Nanholme Mill, Shaw Wood Road
Todmorden OL14 6DA, UK
www.arcpublications.co.uk

978-1-911469-82-7 (pbk)
978-1-911469-90-2 (hbk, subscribers only)

Design by Tony Ward
Printed in Great Britain by TJ Books,
Padstow, Cornwall

The cover photograph is by kind permission of
KL Magazine

ACKNOWLEDGEMENTS
The publishers are grateful to Stephen Stuart-Smith for
granting permission to reproduce poems from the following collections
originally published by Enitharmon Press:
The Language of Yes (1996); *Poems from East Anglia* (1997);
Selected Poems (2001); *Moored Man* (2006);
The Mountains of Norfolk (2011); and *The Breaking Hour* (2015).
They also acknowledge first publication of many of these poems in
The Rain-Giver (Deutsch, 1972), *The Dream-House* (Deutsch, 1976),
Time's Oriel (Hutchinson, 1983), *Waterslain* (Hutchinson, 1986),
The Painting-Room (Hutchinson, 1988),
Attraction Water (The Happy Dragons' Press, 2011) and
Seahenge (Kailpot Press, 2019).

Arc Publications UK & Ireland Series
Series Editor: Tony Ward

My *Collected Poems* includes all the work I have written and wish to keep up to 2025. Founded on my previous *Selected Poems* (2001 and 2011), it also draws on work from *The Breaking Hour* (2015), *Gravity for Beginners* (2021) and the chapbook *Harald in Byzantium* (2022), and more recent poems.

Stephen Stuart-Smith was my publisher at Enitharmon for over twenty years, and I'm most grateful to him for allowing me and Arc Publications to reproduce many poems. My thanks also to friends far and wide for their encouragement, some regular, some occasional, and above all to Lawrence Sail for his help in choosing the work included in my *Selected Poems* (2011).

My wife Linda has given me incisive and loving support and has commented on all my poems, while my P. A. Vikki Powles, at first 'straining in the slips', then working overtime, helped me to produce the final script

And of course I'm indebted to the indefatigable Tony Ward and Angela Jarman, not only for taking aboard this large collection but publishing it in two editions – a hardback for subscribers and a paperback for allcomers.

Kevin Crossley-Holland
Chalk Hill, June 2025

CONTENTS

The Rain-Giver (1972)

THE RAIN-GIVER

DAY

The sky's visor opened: there was a face,
Immense and undefined, bearing down on you
Who staggered round the stairhead, dangerously,
Looking up at the glass, and through the glass,
At the clouds crossing. And you were awed
As the face dissolved in water streams,
Then reformed, better defined, still blurred
By the uneven, eighteenth-century glass.
This I saw, precarious on the cracking slates,
Bucket in hand, cleaning the cupola.
And you called out, a loud, demanding shout,
Perhaps to cover your uncertainty.
You shrank when I replied with reassurances;
My disembodied call reverberated
Down the flights, died shivering in the hall.

NIGHT

There was thunder, somewhere, a long way off
And never nearer, like a gong struck lightly.
Dusk came; you could hear it no longer,
And the rain came, softly – a shadow stealing up
Then rapping at the cupola. 'Rain,'
You called, 'rainrain.' We stood on the stairhead,
Peering into the black, topless hole.
You know he lives there, though you cannot see him.
He hides from you behind a mask of darkness,
The powerful one, the rain-giver. He stands
Behind the panes and smacks them with his hands;
You laugh and acknowledge him again and again.
And now you call out for my attention,
Point out the dark stain which has seeped
Through the cupola, trickles down the wall.

THE WALL

I am a desolate wall, accumulator of lichen.
Men made me with flint chippings and, fickle as always,
ignored me; time did not ignore them.
My business is to divide things: the green ribbons
of grass from the streams of macadam; the kitchen gardens
from the marsh acres, garish with sea-lavender;
the copses of ilex and pine from the North Sea,
the bludgeoning waves of salt water where seabirds play.
I stand grey under the East Anglian sky,
glint when the occasional sun opens its eye.

My business is to divide things, my duty to protect.
I am unrepaired; men neglect me at their own risk.
Time takes me in mouthfuls; the teeth of the frost
bit into my body here; here my mortar crumbles;
the wind rubs salt into every wound.
Elsewhere I am overgrown with insidious ivy;
it wound its arms around me only to strangle me.

Relentless, the sea rolls down from the Pole.
It levelled the dunes last year, removed the marram grass,
clashed its steel cymbals over the marsh and macadam.
It attacked me and undermined me; I sway
like a drunkard now; yet it could not gash me
with its gleaming scythes; it was not strong enough.
I stand, sad, and stare at all this estate,
the lawns, the kitchen gardens, copses garrulous
in the wind. I carefully listen, listen and wait
for the fierce outsider to force his way in.

DUSK, BURNHAM-OVERY-STAITHE

The blue hour ends, this world
floats on a great stillness.

I only guess where marsh
finishes and sky begins,

each grows out of the other.
In the creek a slip

of water gleams. Rowboats
bob and swing above the mud,

the barnacled and broken
ribs of Old Stoker's boat.

A wedge of gulls rustles
overhead, and for a moment

the water notices them.
Such calm is some prelude.

Then across the marsh it comes,
the sound as of an endless

train in a distant cutting,
the god working his way back,

butting and shunting,
reclaiming his territory.

This world's his soundbox now;
in the stillness he still moves.

Anything could happen.

CONFESSIONAL

I come once more to this terrible place;
As it was it is, each stone and each face

Unchanged, making an index of the change
In me. Everything here was arranged

Long ago; the wind, raking from the north,
Saw to that and sees to it. In the hearth

Coals glow and the ash flies early and late;
Every face is ruckled, sands corrugate;

Inland, those superstitious hawthorn trees
Strain away from the wind and heckled seas.

Yet I come. Here alone I cannot sham.
The place insists that I know who I am.

Elemental trinity – earth, air, sea –
Harshly advocate my humility:

You are bigoted, over ambitious,
You are proud, you salute the meretricious.

Then I have altered this much with the years:
That I need more to admit my errors,

From fear, and a longing not to be blind;
So I am scoured by the unchanging wind,

And rid again of some superfluity
By that force uninterested in me.

And I can go, prepared for the possible;
Dream and bone set out from the confessional.

A LINDISFARNE TOMBSTONE

for Eric Elstob

1

Norsemen storm the cells:
The hive ablaze; sluice of blood,
Garnet-bright, under sword and axe;
The golden comb iron reaps;
A knot of monks drone Pax Pax
By candles' light; wax weeps.

A furore Normanorum, libera nos, Domine.

2

Two monks crooked in prayer:
Cuthbert incorrupt and unscathed;
A good haul from Bee Hill;
Quick requital for slaughter;
Freedom from shadows still
Shrithing over the minds' water.

A furore Normanorum, libera nos, Domine.

EPITHALAMIUM

for Stephen and Judy Kane

The sun struck at you where you stood,
still separate, and braced bright bands
around you. It was momentary,
but absolute; then you moved on,
and in your train bridesmaid and page
uncompromised.
                    All down the nave
the congregation, topped and tailed,
was mottled in the light stained glass
had caught, and altered, and passed on;
blotched red and yellow, blue, green, they
sneaked glances at each other, sang
together, watched bride and groom.

Watched and identified: for one
a dream, and one a dream gone wrong,
for one never to come, and one
not even now a dream; and then,
through you, some sense renewed of all
that's possible, always being
unfulfilled.
                    That hot Saturday
in June in a dormitory town,
the purpose of a pilgrimage:
we gazed at your coincidence,
that where you stood, by some good chance
light fell unstained and married you.

THE ISLAND

Seven days, seven nights in a place of stone:
Atlantic anvil where winds and water hone
Men to what they are, long bundles of bone.

Seven days, seven nights in a place of stone
Where each man learns he is at last alone,
So quickly comes to love, forgive, condone.

Seven days, seven nights in a place of stone.
Saffron flowers in the fissures are soon grown
To all they can become: each one its own

Spirit's song, momentary wild laughter thrown
Against grey walls, the grey sky, the grey sea.

The Dream-House (1976)

FORTIFICATION

for Barry and Maggie

Gat-toothed grey hill.
                        Another encampment,
Another whorl of escarpments, bulging
And vital.
                Eyes at the interstices,
Regular, round as compasses and clocks;
And behind ramparts, hidden from without,
Orderly mounds of slingstones, small forests
Of ash-spears, sunstruck shields and bodyguards,
All the gear, ready.
                        Within the enclosure
A mill of herded humans with livestock,
A concourse with no air of business
As usual, wholly abandoned.
                                They pound
The fort's last grassblade flat, voluntary
Prisoners in their own windy village,
Settled on their hidebound plans, old and young
With horses and cattle, pigs, hens.
                                        Distance,
Middle distance, blur and definite small
Knots dislocate from the tangle, make off
And hole up in their huts.
                            Squalls, grunts and shouts
Begin to sound singular, the last out
Hurry as if they have to.
                            Enter night
From all sides, a sudden flurry of wind
Like the wind of the dead rustles and leaves
The arena empty.
                    I could no more
Ignore the challenge here than journey close
To my birthplace and ignore it; I have
A white handkerchief, a quiver of needs
I cannot flight.

    Climber in the blue hour
To the contour of an answer.
      Wanting
Further admission, a password-seeker,
Poking round, following lines of small hills
Moles have thrown up, and shortly before dark
Emerging from the compound, both pockets
Stuffed with sherds.
      Nothing sharply specified,
But in some way reassured, half-defined,
Apprehending again there may never
Be clear questions, pointed, but simply this
Returning need settled by communion:

Traveller, peaceable, until the next bend.

IN THE COMPANY OF SAINTS

It was my only meeting with that man.
Glad of his van's noise that half-justified
Our silences, we jolted out of Cleggan
And, under the banked and glaring sky,

Bruised across miles of rubbed sand to Omey.
We stumbled through deep dunes there, immense shoals
That shift entirely when Malin's under siege,
And came as if by chance to an incorrupt hollow.

The latest storms had resurrected at our feet
Pink keystones and the tops of walls – the church
Of a small saint unmentioned in dictionaries
And Calendars. The bright light pronounced

Each granite block a perfect fit, the gable-ends
Truly cut, unmarred in a millennium.
The place looked almost ready for service,
As if at any moment we would hear

Fechin and his monks singing God's praises,
Recrossing the spit. Conscious of years shared,
The generous experience of that sanctuary,
We settled on one bank. But then that man

Swiftly turned the talk from wonder, told me
Of double death – our friend and her daughter.
With such care he chose the time, the place
Which partly transmuted that horror into myth.

Their lives and deaths seemed one with ours;
Kneeling there in the company of saints, it seemed
We could contain and ride and redeem them: a shock
Immediate yet at once remote, as it is now.

THE FIRST ISLAND

There it was, the island.

Low-slung sandhills like land-waves, fettered by marram.
One hut, a dark nugget. Across the creeks gleaming like
tin, like obsidian, across the marshes almost rust,
olive, serge, fawn, purpled for a season, the island.

We shoaled on the Staithe, stared out and possessed it;
children who collar half the world with a shout, and
share it in a secret.

Old men sat on a form lodged against the wall.
Of course we did not ask. We knew. They were too old.

There it was, and at times not there. Atmosphere
thickened, earth and air and water became one lung;
we were in a wilderness.

In a coat of changing colours it awaited us. In the
calm seas of our sleep it always loomed, always ahead.
We woke, instantly awake. As if we never had been
tired, and all things were possible.

So the boat came for us. The island stretched out to
us and we took it for granted. And no one asked by
which creeks we had come or could return.

RAPIDS

1

'Of course I will not go. I will be here.
Of course I'll still be here, I promise you.'
It is enough, I can still reassure
Them with words true now, not for tomorrow.
So they go off for conkers, shout, and fire
For unripe high-fliers; they break a bough...

What is there we do not wound with our touch?
My two sons, I cannot love you too much.

2

All afternoon he talked about that bridge
Through Salisbury, Stockbridge, Basingstoke and Staines.
The pressure of things we did not manage,
Tears suppressed, issues skirted like towns...
We reached peeling London, parted, climbed, dodged
Pedestrians like unexploded mines,

Ran back towards each other. It was his cue.
'Can't you stay tonight? Please stay. Why must you...

3

Don't keep asking. Let him open the door.
He is entitled to his privacy.
Isn't it enough for him to endure
This going, is it so necessary
To thrash it all out? No, he must first dare
Himself, the rapids of his misery.

This is a test of love. Leave him alone.
He is not mine, or hers: he is his own.

CLEAN MONDAY, RAMNOUS

A fallen streamer rustles and sidles
Across the floor. After each guest and gust
The door slams; a youngest daughter bridles
At some strange hungry smile, and in the dust

Outside, the hens scatter at the clatter
To the rough yard's corners, nettles, the fence.
Their loss is that nothing does not matter:
Assiduous devotees of nonsense,

They peck at grit and small chips of marble
And ignore the field's red lips across the road
Where the man waits. The swirling winds garble
His shouts, translate them into ode, then goad.

His girl hears, rises; again the door slams.
He carries a kite – an eagle or buzzard.
With skill he hoists it, plays it, now it runs
And climbs further before blast and blizzard.

Then his daughter takes it. When it tugs, dives,
She shrieks with such excited fear, aware
Of ravening beyond her, and of lives
She could live that have not yet escaped her.

So she yields, he resumes. Hand over hand
He holds the line just as he grasps his spade.
This one day he abandons the land;
He forgets the vine, the growing green blade,

His taverna's patrons, already tight.
He is washing off the soil of the year,
Acknowledging Lachesis. The great kite
Is like a tongue preying on air, a prayer.

PETAL AND STONE

An old antithesis: petal and stone.
There were anemones near that valley site,
Furled up against such freezing wind. They alone
Looked living in that mottled place – blood-bright.

She dropped to her knees by a brilliant small
Colony, carefully selected one,
And leaned back against a rock. That was all
It seemed, but it could have been a lion:

Only the torso, and that mauled by time,
But still the defiant cold lord of the land.
She stretched out against it, so tender, feline:
The flower had opened to wilt in her hand.

THE DREAM-HOUSE

My eyes are sore. They sting with my own salt.
This day I have been the fetch of the sea.

Those shapes are round and kind yet fast as rocks.
What are their names? I must think of their names.

They speak firm words in soft ways. I like it
When they speak, and when they sit with no words.

Look at him, then. Look at him. John, John, John,
Once more a small wee boy, old bag of bones.

At your head the wax burns and Christ stares down
From the Cross. It is all just as it was

When you were a child and I was a child,
Each on our own in the long dark. You seem

To sleep as I would. No, it is not that,
Or it is that but more than that. I look

And you are not tired and not sad; you are calm
As the swell of the slow deep sea in June.

All you were in your time smiles as you meet,
Like a long lost friend, the end of all time.

First James now John in six months. So I am
The last one. Soon he must leave his clean sheets,

His bed, for the press of earth on the lid.
What are these? Why do I cry tears once more?

My sleeve is as rough as a tom cat's tongue.
Do not look at me. I am troughs and waves.

What is that noise? That noise? A gale of laughs
From young men and girls that sit at the hearth.

Where do they think they are? This is a wake,
Not a dance hall. They grin and nudge and wink.

John, John, John, this is your wake. I will stand
When I can and throw the pack of them out.

This is your wake, not a dance hall. No, no,
I am wrong. Let it be as it should be.

Let there be smoke from pipes, the games and songs.
They are his friends who chose to come and choose

To stay as long as this long night. We were
The same, quick in our words and ways, our blood.

What is the time? The priest will come with prayers,
Then the day with wind, tears. It will be done.

Your will be done. John, John, John, I will clean
The lamp in your room as if you were here.

VISION

Watch me if you want to.
I'm as shifty as a daddy-long-legs
on a polished pane.
You are where I was
and you will never catch me.

Why do you never tire of me?
Is it simply that I am
always beyond you,
all but indiscernible,
air trembling before rain?

I am your pursuit,
your thirst, your one thought;
only the mirage
that only will refresh you.
Watch me (if you want to).

GLUM'S WARPING

Remember the way west up over Hrafkel's land?
The path string-thin, sorry as a sheep run,
Out of his shieling and into Shut Wood?
Men called that the mossmen's track.
Year after year we used to climb it,
Pairs or small groups strapped with panniers,
Until the troll-terror… True?
Listen to this, and you will not need ask.
See my old hand: with hammer-sign
And sign of cross I swear it so.

Glum Gunnarson ganged up with me.
(He turned many heads, handsome,
Fearless, eager for fame. On his account
Married women wished they were widows
And single girls slept uncertainly.)
It was July. Just after dawn
We met and, chewing mastic, made
Our way through Shut Wood. After that,
A short cut beneath Shouting Cliff
And so we reached the moss rafts under the glacier.

For ten seconds I'd turned my back,
Having a piss. Imagine this:
Glum was straining every sinew, racing
Up towards the glacier; and there, ghastly
On an icy spur, sat a troll-
Woman, waiting. Ugly and gigantic,
With huge, crossed hands she beckoned him.
'Glum! Glum!' I yelled. No good.
He buried himself in her breast without a backward glance
And she loped away over the ice.

The dear man was mourned in Blafell,
He was missed at the Allthing. People thought
The ogress might rub him with ointment – as one
Rubbed Thorvald thirty years ago –
And stretch him, and shout into his ears,
Trying to turn him into a troll.
And no grey-haired man at all gave Glum
The least change of escaping the giantess

If he had licked her ladle; they said
His fate would be to fare the fells always.

Summer, autumn, the usual antiphon,
Then the dirge of winter: we lit candles
For Glum, hopeless, yet grim and hoping.
The next spring two shepherds –
I was out from Iceland, south over sea –
They found Glum at the foot of the glacier,
Tatterdemalion. With cries and tears
They greeted him. One asked, 'Are you still man?'
The other: 'What do you believe in?'
'God,' growled Glum and at once stumped away.

Next summer solstice I saw him myself,
My friend, gruesome, with a growth of hair for clothing,
Savagely he scowled as he shrithed from the glacier;
He was so surly, a fimbul-fambi with no tongue,
And yet he stayed by me – what was he thinking?
Of girls with fair tresses, friendship in Blafell?
'Glum Gunnarson, what do you believe in?'
'Trunt, Trunt,' he grunted. 'Trunt,
And the trolls in the fells.' He guffawed and stalked off,
Gone for ever. That is the end of the story.

Time's Oriel (1983)

THE MONK'S REFLECTIONS

Too much consistency: at last I dared
Kick the comfortable restraints, the bells'
Gentle hubbub, fraternal silences,
Dispersals and reunions. All our
Observances, the Rule, had become soft
With regiment and custom: time to change.

This is what I tried to think, partly thought,
Repeated so often because I had
Still to convince myself; then I kissed all
My brethren and under my skin hurried
To the spines of breakers, growling and grey-green,
The bucking ocean. My heart was aching.

I wanted to negotiate my own
Way to heaven, a crash course hazardous
With iceberg and whale: glass mountains that sing
Of how they will mother what mothered them;
Fastitocalon, apparent island
Who sinks the unwary anchored on him.

So for love I sailed north. Guided by God,
Wind-guardian, I left the secret glades,
The salmon streams, and crossed the bitter sea
Until I was driven to this loveless
Extremity. And, even now, I do
Not know the name of this icy cauldron.

This is my cell of the senses: time counts
In here and I count it – for each day
One stroke on that stripped log, and each full moon
A striation. My knife itself is pared
Like bark or rind. Five years, and rows of days...
Only God can tell how many longer.

And in that small cell, with its sky-ceiling,
I celebrate the offices. *O God,*
Seven times a day do I praise thee. At
Midnight I will rise and give thanks to thee.
Between boulders I pray, and between
Prayers cultivate crops and fantasies.

For how can I forget her, Grania,
Her flaming eyes? I cannot help my dreams.
I'm a rack-wretch, even now unable
To forget her, unable to flatten
The mind's fenders and remember clearly.
Even these words...

Your voice had to do with the bees; your eyes
Were on fire. Do you think of that green glade,
The sun behind the leaves, the leafy bed?
Do you think about those oaths, made and broken?
How did you look? And how do you look now?
Your oval face I saw in every face,

From which, after all, there is no escape?
I thought it was right to come, and maybe
It was right, but I should have explained it.
At least that. Now I cannot undo it,
And even if in time you understood,
You will have branded me lover-coward.

Life around me as my body withers:
The timeless stream of all things that are born
And do die, all children of one mother.
I am peaceful at times, incorporate;
Then the sublime whole shatters, and each part
Translates her, it embodies Grania.

I single out a sweet pattern of stars,
Her configuration in the chill air,
She is that remote light on the mountain,
This brown-eyed flower. Each is an ambush,
A torturer divine; for though I live –
In labour, prayer, shifting dream – I seem now

To live only through these incarnations.

CHILDREN IN THE CHERRY TREE

They perch in the cherry tree – two fledglings
Not quite hidden, gigglers in the dusk, hatching a plan.
The tree begins to shake them. It is not laughing,
It groans, its limbs beat slowly like prehistoric wings
And skin-soft leaves, yellow and pink and red, cascade.

So high and so cold, the tree now such a stranger.

Peering out from their eyrie, and down through the web
Of branches, the silent high-riders hear shouts
In their throats. Their colours are lowered, dashes
Of scarlet and white legging it down as light fails,
As darkness lopes along the waiting blue hills.

GRANDMOTHER'S FOOTSTEPS

No to the birds no to the flowers no to the sprinkler
All washing the garden with soft water colours
As the sun goes down. No to the friends presents
Cakes candles laughter. It is as if they were not
And had never been. Alone she stands at one end
Of the lawn facing all that does not matter
Only aware of that dark tunnel behind her.

As the shapes approach stealthy and insistent
Steps of the smilers silent and murderous
She clenches her teeth her fists her limbs almost lock
And she stares into the darkness. But there
Is still so much she can do with sheer vigilance
For so long for as long as her mind body her own will
Do not work against her. There! And there!
In her straightjacket she jerks twists round
'You and you and Ivan you Sally and you
I saw you moving almost all of you.'
Laughing they troop back to the starting-line most of them
But no not all those other ones how long will it be?

The garden is hushed at sundown it is breathless
And the blooms burn to ashes. She knows they must get her
In the end they must let that be soon now.
As if only it were not a deadly serious game
How gladly she would let the first last shape touch her
And even embrace it weeping from such weariness
And relief. But as it is she turns and turns…

NIGHT FLIGHT OUT OF ENGLAND

Already alien: a shining pictograph I can't decipher.
And then a gold settlement not quite as regular
As polka dots; solitaries like stars fallen,
Or just night lights on landings, so dim and forever;
Spokes shooting from a hub that's greenish and ethereal,
Tangents, rhomboids, all that matter made material;
And then the last arrested flash, a scimitar of light,
And I am in the dark; and rising still, still rising,
Quickening to prospects beyond the darkness, look back
Almost lovingly at the land's concealed depressions,
Those seeming patterns, the whole bright bag of tricks.

AN APPROACH TO THE MARSH

The rope is almost paid out here. Bawdeswell
and the ghost of its foul reeve left to stew,
I drive down cool green naves, and soon the lanes
begin to ripple. More pilgrims are shuffled off
to the shrine at Walsingham, and that is an end
to the firm ground of conviction. This is no man's land
that never belongs to earth or sea entirely:
now the flowing barley hemmed by screaming poppies,
a gull perched on a salt-rusted ploughshare
and a gull, a litter of blood-tarred feathers,
festering. A veil of butterflies, opalescent,
dips and quivers and rises, and I come to where
there is no going beyond.
                              Marsh, mud, shifting sand,
creeks sinuous and shining, they look sucked
and rendered almost certain by the sun;
but now and then, and for no evident reason,
rigging yaps, or seabirds shriek at what we cannot
even see, or the sea broadcasts over the marsh...
This bleached boat, that dabber, those children
gathering samphire, leaping over sun-crazed pulks:
the staithe today rests on its August oars;
hard light gives an edge to all that's apparent,
where nothing is what it seems or not for long.

MOSQUITO

Silent fizzer, sting white in the sunlight,
arrowing through air-tides –

                    no sooner said
than you suspect and circle a target
or drift sideways into shadow, unassailable.

A splinter of man's own irritation,
you were here in the beginning,
grinding your teeth.
                  Not much more
than your own appetite, you pick locks
as you please and are skilled at escape.
You weave out of corners, fade before lunges,
Houdini of the darkening straits.

But you come back for more. Disengagement
cannot be your tactic.
                This is a war-game
and ends only with blood's scintilla.
Or no, does not end at all. Abroad,
and under the fan: the shades of your autograph
walk all day across my prickling skin.

SOUTH-WEST MONSOON

The eyelids of a dreaming man; the subtle
Swift movement of a trout into shadow
Or is it the white shift of water itself.
Ripple and flicker, flicker and ripple,
The far-off lightning makes its connections
In the skull. It is very peaceful.
There are no reports. As if the war
Were conducted tonight on some other front.

      As it was then… a malt in my hand
      (Especially shipped for the English Club),
      A trichinopoli, and a verandah,
      Not an infernal pink-and-muggy room.
      Boys waiting in the shadows… damn them!
      They even move like shadows of themselves.
      I'll sit in my cane before this flickering
      Screen, prepared for what may not ever come.

Dazed brass gleams like a fallen moon:
A girl with a waterpot on her head
Walks her liquid walk up the rustling road,
She is sizing the world under her soles.
If she stopped to think, she could tell
Nothing has changed since the beginning.
Aching limbs, sweet water from the well,
Aching limbs… A mongrel howls…

      Every four seconds the needle dances
      And the scape is scalded. Plantains leap
      Out of Dravidian dark, the compound of huts,
      The coarse thatching of coconut palm, old men
      At the thresholds. No one moves.
      No one has ever moved. At times like this
      You could stuff the whole bloody scene
      And no one would know the difference.

The cool tones of the wind's announcement:
Then rain, sheet rain, smacks the glazed face
Of the hotel. In a hundred frames
The sheet glass rocks and holds. The world contracts.
Beyond the panes not even one smear of light,

A kerosene star; the whole compound wiped out.
A Noah's Ark full of grateful prisoners,
The hotel buckets into the darkness.

> Yes, I remember… the bluster, the dark wave
> That hoisted us on to its shoulder.
> 'Batten the hatches! Batten the hatches!'
> Nothing to do but sit and sweat it out,
> The lizards watching the dancing mosquitoes;
> The eyes of the boys, molten, secretive;
> The winking eye of malt; eye of the storm;
> The bungalow bleared, a drowning eye.

Seep and trickle first, pool under the window,
A wound superficial and easily dressed;
But then water wells under the crooked door
And boys hurry in with cloths and containers.
The breach is made, though, the body imperilled.
Fabric and form, what is not at risk
In time of these rains that hammer at the house
Of the active man, the house of the head?

NEENIE

in memory of F. I. M. Crossley-Holland

Under the cowl, out on Scolt Head
The swell and swash are inching their way back.
The water picks up pebbles, razor shells,
Birds' small bleached bones and witches' purses;
It toys with them, cries over them,
And the legendary wave embraces them.

The tide returning: each wave and whisker,
Everything forged into one force,
A fusion with one meaning and purpose.
But I think you are going further,
Ancient shuffler, at the fire now, flushed
By this last blaze before going to bed.

Out of the dark they come at a knobbled wave,
Processions unblemished and undeterred
By time's strictures. Here is the hall
At Oakwell: *The chimney always roars like this;*
Frank is still up in the organ gallery,
Puffing his cigar, blowing out another hymn.

The wind, more wind, and the cottage
Rocks like a boat, quite safe, out at sea.
Remember the train we took up to Wengen
When you were six and I was sixty?
It rocks, nurse, it rocks. I love this nursery.
Kevin, have you met my pregnant sister?

And now there is rain, ripping against the window
(Long since painted into its frame)
Behind the curtain of faded red velvet.
What will become of the passion flowers?
Still, the borders of this tapestry are teeming
With forget-me-knots. I had three proposals...

It goes on and on. You make associations
As children and poets do, bony fingers
Clamped to the sill now, eyes watering:
Not only the tide flowing and gathering up
As it goes, not only time defused,
But for itself a parade of whatever mattered

And for whatever reason, a statement
Risen clear of interest and argument.
I listen and think you are telling something
Greater than its parts, a breath and sum
Of life itself, the ego dispossessed.
Grandmother, sleep, and sleep in peace.

A WREATH

for Edmund

The furled cypress contains it. The breathless yew. Hulks of elms all over England.

A trail of shadows, everywhere, in the oblique sunlight. Who does not accept them? Who is not even grateful for them?

But when the bud...

Not one sound can be undone. It is part of the harmony of the gong.

Look at the water. It sways, catches chips of light, flashes, sways.

Yet snared by time, all of us, that part of us...

Not one stone, one leaf, one flame, one breath. Whatever begins is eternal.

Where he lies now a moonstone lies, one with flint and chert and every granule of earth.

And the darkness comprehendeth it not...

A moonstone on her throbbing hand. Light in the stone, life's pointer. Brother of the hawthorn, the wood-anemone, the breathing iridescent universe.

IN DORSET AND WILTSHIRE

for Sally and Dick

1

In the blue hour definitions and distances
Become undecided; the cantering fields
Shimmer with light caught and reluctantly yielded.
First to retreat are the barrows strung out along
The hilltop, cropped and lop-sided but still
To be reckoned with. They gather the darkness
Back into themselves and they emit darkness –
Day's dying reminder – as their builders intended.

2

If night air thickens and unknowing clouds of mist
Weep and wrap round the cathedral, its floodlights
Seem more powerful; drowned in light, the spire
Rises a second time, a dim delineation
Above itself, disembodied and floating.
Matter illumines spirit, illusion appears miracle:
Darkness disinherited, light begetting light
By which chiefly I see how much I cannot see.

DRAGON

for Gillian

Swirling fire-drake astride the northern skies,
Fafnir, Knucker and Serpent of Henham,
Muckle Mester Stoor Worm and Civic Snap:

Bless your sister sprung in human form,
Let this girl with a storm of flaming hair
Be abundant as a dragon from the orient,

A house-guardian, a bringer of rain.

Sigurd and Beowulf, George, Carantoc,
Seigneur de Hambrye, Shonks and Assipattle:
Turn protectors now with your massive shields

And your spiked war-gear, your poison and fire.
She will be ruler of the inner kingdom.
I say she is worthy of all your care

And the light armour of a poet's words.

POSTCARDS FROM KODAI

Here I am once more. Do you remember
the castanets of toads at dusk, thousands
of them? The veil, diaphanous, that drifts
over the glaze of the five-fingered lake?
This will bring it back if anything will.
Colonel Edgcumbe is here again and sends
regards – we two are the last survivors.

*

Have you ever stood higher than the clouds
and watched them smoking, lifting from valleys?
This is the eyrie of the Western Ghats.
From the verandah of this bungalow
I can survey the whole apparent world,
everything, my dear, trapped in place or time,
hazy or shining. Godlike, powerless!

*

Down at the Carlton the new head waiter
is called Joseph! Is that a requirement
for the post? They still fold all the napkins
in unexpected ways and trick them out with
wildflowers. A log fire in the grate
and, outside, the cool air close with pinesmoke,
the improving smell of eucalyptus
(only this would seem the least out of place
in an Alpine resort). Dear old Kodai!
There are changes here, but not as elsewhere.

*

You'd laugh, Emily. The Carlton Hotel –
I went there for tea with Colonel Edgcumbe –
still has the books we combed through as children:
Just Patty, True Tilda and *Bawbee Jock*.
Does that ring a bell or two? They're wrapped now
in parcel paper, and kept behind glass.
As if they were quite irreplaceable.

*

Big changes in the air at the golf club!
A 'high water rise tank and sump' have been
installed; they mean to replace all the browns
with greens. What was good enough for us...
But no, they must always go one better.
It all seems a dreadful waste of money.
Are these the highest golf links anywhere?
I asked the new secretary but he does
not know. Typical! Hope this card gets through!

*

Light is a generous discoverer.
Like God, it finds itself. The sleeping lake
wakes, stretches, slips into its newfound shape
as if all its life had been the darkness
of dream and illusion. A countenance
liquid, empty, impassive; one bird sings...'

*

I can't quite explain it but I feel free
to ride my own tides: it is a certain
glory in all my thoughts and emotions,
the ego's representatives. They are
my coat of many colours on this earth.
The same force that fathers inhibition
and denial changes course within me:
here I can become the song of myself.

*

You'd think little or nothing of the sound
of rain falling on outstretched leaves, falling
from leaf to leaf. You hear it every day
almost. But this soft rainmusic, my dear,
always at my ear with how it will be,
how it was: this is really why I come
to this dreaming hill station. I suppose
it is the nearest I will get to home.

AT FIESOLE

Time dies as the light fails.

Tulips of tungsten signal to bats
On their flight-paths; a dog barks
Itself hoarse; the cypresses
Continue to hold their breath.

Whatever happens is elsewhere:
The huddled hilltop towns, below

And indigo; the aureate city.

Through the thyme-rich air hanging
In the dark lane, a pair of fireflies
Dance letters of light... they are
Spelling out an enchanted story.

Your breath warm on my breath,
Your breath on the sweet night air.
Time dies as the light fails.
Once upon a time and ever after.

Waterslain (1986)

from **WATERSLAIN**

On the Dyke

Years back,
still on the first green leg
a boy walks side by side
with his fair-haired younger sister.

How earnestly they talk!
How little they miss the world
between us!
They've ambushed almost half the tribe out
in the slant sunlight!

I can hear their voices
far off and very clear…
For as long as I watch
they come on towards me.

Laddie first, riddling
mussels on the Hard,
and Fred stepping out with a good-looking dame,

then down to the dark pools tepid
and chill,
Diz dabbing for her supper.

They corner St Vitus,
eager for spoils,
advance on laughing Agnes…
pass up luckless Bodge.

At the first elbow
they begin to frisk and shout;
they scramble, somersault,
vault this whole embankment

first breached and sandbagged in the Great Flood,
forgetful once more
under wild rose, silverweed, spurrey.

A wave from the Warden
and they're out on their own again…

It's afternoon and slant
and of all places in England
I walk here today,

Mrs Riches

A screw of peardrops
ready for each milk-white child
arrived late
last night from miles inland.

Through the gloom
in that low-slung stockpiled room
proofed with boxes
her growl conspiratorial:

'Owd Billie's gone.'
'Sin what Vic ploughed up?'
'McCullough's buyin' into Hunst'n.'
'Vitus found a walrus.'

And that once, horrified,
leaning right across her counter:

'Foive at Heacham
and Wilkie's houseboat wedged
up East Harbour Way
and that owd MTB
dumped on the quay at Wells
and sin the sandbags
and first owd Arthur knew was water
through his keyhole…'

No tale, not even this,
quite all told
in this spiced corner of paradise,
the bell always being rung.

Diz

Easterlies have sandpapered her larynx.

Webbed fingers, webbed feet:
last child of a seal family.

There is a blue flame at her hearth, blue
mussels at her board.
Her bath is the gannet's bath.

Rents one windy room at the top of a ladder.
Reeks of kelp.

'Suffer the little children,' she barks
and the children – all the little ones –
are enchanted.

She has stroked through the indigo of
Dead Man's Pool
and returned with secrets.

They slip their moorings. They
tack towards her glittering eyes.

Billy

Every year a new draft,
this buoy replanted, this groyne halfdismantled,
the Cockle Path patched up,
and the Mouth itself narrower, wider...
For how, since Ararat,
can earth or sea ever be satisfied?

He knows these creeks inch by inch,
their silt and shining, their dark complexities,
and when to shoulder the Rosemary into action,
veterans both of Dunkirk.

'C'mon, then, me bootie!'
Infirm and elderly and eager young
he hands from jetty into bows,

a salt shepherd
gentling doubts, winking at such high hopes.

Eyes pale blue, say lace agate,
as the North Sea never is.
Eyes that on a clear day
see over a thousand scrolls
to the end of the world.

Diddakoi

The wheel of swart water
noiseless
that whirls above the dead, retracted eye;

and the spiked piers that never
impaled Hitler,
still hungry for landings;

the four cracked sails,
shining whore berries
and on Gun Hill the frayed red flag;

and Joan
with her duff pegs and sunset scarf –
not her light
fingers or wide hips

but the craft,
the blood,
and the patterns on the sands
before the tide absolved them:

in the same black breath
speak them.

Bodge

He is their cracked mirror
and the boys don't like what they can see:

the work of a cruel caricaturist –
a boneless dumpling
who grins too long and blubs too much,
upper lip always damp with snot or sweat.

Elbowed out of their secret councils,
their expeditions
cockling, crabbing, cycling the lost lanes,
he teaches them their cruelty.

And on the beach alone
under the sky's awnings,
shy of the sea's claws,
he gives back their sense of loneliness.

Pink and fluttering and maimed:
seldom, they discover, can the tongue sing
just what the heart means.

Bloated windsock, crumpling.

Only later do they come on
the Christian virtues.
In the mirror each face suffers a smile.

Shuck

From saucer pulks
where pale light lingers longest
we made his eyes.

In this seedbed only think:
Dead Hands wave, Things worm,
marsh lights flicker.

We made his blood from arteries
obsidian in the moonlight,
his hair from shaggy sea-purslane.
His chains are chains of marsh mist.

Skriker, Hooter, Fenrir:
these are his blood-brothers.
We gave him the howl of wind
carried from Siberia.

And witnesses?
With terror or with damp black
earth, one way or another
he stops every mouth.

Beachcomber

Faithful as a wordfisher,
there he goes, old magpie of the foreshore!
Face chafed and chapped like driftwood.

Parcelled shapeless against
winds straight off the icecap
but look! agile even so, jumpy as a tick,
quick in his pickings.

Scoofs along the tideline scurf,
his oily sack full of consonants:
hunks of wax,
and seacoal, rubber ballast, cork,
sodden gleanings.

And swinging in that shoe-bag hitched
to his broad belt?
Ah! In there, sunlight and amber moonlight,
emerald and zinc and shell-pink,
Aegir's vowels.

The Great Painter

Though his spirit
possesses that house as surely as
violet shades course through the creek,
shutters blind the windows from month to month
and salt cancers the royal blue.

He has escaped to sweets
at St Columb, and Paris and Provence,
a plump indulgent wavelength
of pink and crimson, viridian, ultramarine.

The lines here are too Lutheran:
flat-chested dunes,
the ruled horizontals of marsh and ocean.

Too near the bone!
He shuddered when the wind's mouth framed
its forbidding questions.

Not for him
light honed on a northern whetstone,
the burning ice of aurora borealis;
nor was he the first to flinch
at this ruthless incandescence,
too cutting even for Crome and Cotman,
still awaiting a master.

Caretaker

When the tarmac's in a sweat
and Poker's field is waterslain,
his leafy books curl up like shrimps.

That serves him right.
The staithe needs life, not furriners,

only
so little life is left:
nothing but dregs up Norton Creek
once ploughed by shingle boats and whelkers,
black silt over landing stages,
a poor crop
of children unlikely to stay.

It's the same with half his class:
no thought except for Number One.
They would've pumped
not sucked
if this place were not a plaything
but their heartbeat.

Old fule!
You can squeeze his bleeding walls.
Dry, I write. *Dry*.

Local Historian – a found poem

A low flat coastline, sand and saltmarsh;
and a streak of light,
bright as fish scales...

Up to 100 tons, malt, coal, corn and oil-cake;
the great granaries and maltings
all converted...

Ceased to be
cruciform. Mutilated; mutilated;
now form the Brothercross
on the little green below the church.
Squat, crouching tightly;
the wind sweeping in from the sea...

Paid for destroying of Jackdaws;
Paid Gam Gregory
for spreading the mould in the churchyard;
Payd to Joseph Bobbit for a Book
which is concerned with distemper which now rages
amongst the horned cattle;
Paid for 12 Jackdoyes (jackdoyes 3 a 1d.)...

A very gruesome story:
in the year 1307
William Umphrey, chaplain, and Robert de Orleyns
boarded his ship,
bound his hands behind his back until
the blood gushed out at the nails,
imprisoned him until...

As a boy Horatio Nelson;
a short cut through the churchyard;
the headstones bear many names still very familiar –
Woodget, Parr, Haines, Scoles, Riches, Thompson,
Mason...
Have gone; remain; in spite of; whirlpools;
think; walk; rustles;
windows.

Wildfowler

Seven sounds in the pallor.

The sound of the silent assassin –
a slice of white moon
between his teeth.

The sound of no-wind,
nothing but pressure in the silent frame.

Then sleeping water,
not stertorous or small-sighing,
still lost in some dark sliding dream.

The mutter on the marsh
and at once its antiphon –
Banjo's shallow breathing.

Now it comes,
the thickening of air,
the rush of wings
and passionate sky-voices:
a spring of teal,
then mallard, jinking redshank, widgeon.

The No. 4 out of the Magnum.

Great clump on the marsh, splash in the creek,
and Banjo's off !

– All before the opening
of day's intricate soundbox.

Vic

Stirs; quite delicately sips;
yawns over Friday's yellowed *Advertiser*...

Outside is cold as inside
is cold, wind flights over the marsh,
the walls of the sky drip

as Vic already rises,
eases himself out, pink and primed,

into the beginning –
shapes still inchoate,
pewter on oyster, seacoal on zinc.
Time never was for pondering.

Banjo far-off on the brew!
A taste of plickplack in the air!
No smell of sharp rain!
His sense of day is animal
and utterly secure.

Crossing the yard,
he gossips
with passerines in the thistle scrub;
hails and cajoles the two Suffolks
(the black gelding and chestnut mare)
into the shafts...

Didn't you see his wading walk?
That almost inward smile?
He is this land's stage manager –

dawn corrugator,
trawler of a thousand screaming gulls –

overseer
in the candid light
watching you for one moment
longer
than you watched him.

   John

Unlike that *shiten shepherde* down the road,
his staff is duty, his smocking
self-effacement,
as if he thinks to keep his head
well down might enable his flock to win
a better view of God.

Time has not incised his face but moulded it.

After the Black Death's lapping,
the sea's recession:
oyster-men and salt-men and samphire-gatherers,
they all followed
the singing tideline,
turned their backs on this flint hulk
(thirty years and still unfinished)
in the lee of the hill.

Not lost in the mind's labyrinth –
unmoved by the sophistry of disputation,
the ecstasy of mystics –
but always on the road, spinning
round his parishes 'held in plurality',
year by year he has sought
to narrow that old gap between
man and God.

His slow smile is part of God's promise.

'Listen' he says. 'Only listen.'
He listens in prayer,
as vacant as his beaten church
circled by spirits of wind.
He listens to the Word –
King James' tidal cadences
that follow the heart's contours.

There was a man sent from God...

Miss McQueen

Gong Lane and greengages:
this morning in the orchard
I coached myself and coaxed myself
to walk alone
again:

application gets you so far.
Could've! Should've!

I never realized.
Sometime mistress of parabola and paradox,
almost finished, schooling cabbages.

This one body…

And now you bring me
flagrant poppies

and yes I know
John will come with communion later.

Reproofs! Consolations!
When all I see
is splayed legs, still coltish,
eyes bright in their bone stoups,
one last refusal.

Laddie

King
of the small pool.
Trooper, tussler, accruer, custodian.

Watchful and terse
as the luminous cat-tide rises
and *Duck* and *Golden* swing
then straighten
on their anchors – his engines
fuelled
on whelks and summer passengers.

The black shingle barges: his.
The mussel lays: his.
Silvermilk slakes won by Several Order.
And when the water drops back
and drains, he tracks trespassers
with huge binoculars.

Horsewhipped at thirteen.
Brought an action against the farmer.

Rowed provisions under fire
across the Tigris.

A salty word; the snick of a smile;
in no way prodigal
but English and not to be crossed.

And now
he is watching,
holding court and watching
as this spring tide still rises,
creeps through the marsh,
floods the capillaries,

until there is such a shining
as far as far Trowland and Scolt Head,
unbroken
to the line of the sallow wave.

Tertiary

Down a lane holm-oaks
hallow, all but islanded by drifts
stocky and immaculate –
snowdrop, anemone, marguerite –
Old Agnes flourishes.

Seasoned perennial,
rubicund and rotund, always affable,

she leads pilgrims out
to the green hollow
(earth springy, then giving)
and the silent ferment sweet to the tongue,
the nipples flowing.

'Here is the canal
the poor souls row down to get provisions…'
Suffused with lily pads and bulrushes.

'This is the aching arch
of departure and return…'
Grey-green with lichen, crumbling.

'And here is their Dormitory…'
Stones for pillows.

So very little reason
why they should not be
here, white habits, white cowls,
thronging this place.

    Furriner

That rumpus on the staithe,
all that flap and hoisting
as the tide rises;
reunions at the Moorings;
coronas of light in the quiet houseboats:

you
may call it artificial,
this summer respiration;
I say the place choked on its own silt.

On the rocks, was it?

Every month another
shell for the wind to moan in...

What is unnatural
is this shoal of shiny Midlanders,
traipsing and sinal.
Not ratty, we call them.

Just as it is, was it?

No, when I round the bend
in the scalding lane
and see that immense, almost-empty theatre –
breathing marsh,
signals of the sea –

I say I have reached home.

Leaving

On this tall dyke
where I have walked and watched
there was a meeting.

Under the fizzing hard blue light
you must narrow your eyes at,
generations dovetailed
and half the village quickened:

gossip's sharp spindrift first,
then those considerations that seldom
trouble children – dark tides
tugging at every anchorage in the creek.

It grew late...

It was my own children
leaped from me,
looking in all directions.
They surge down this lifeline
here and now
towards the gold ramparts
and the skirling sea,

and still, high over them and me
and the sea-acres, the land-acres,
the gulls criss-cross
like stitches, like nets, like arguments,
like love.

WOMAN SORTING REDCURRANTS

Her back is still straight but
her eyes are bleeding.
Through the honeysuckle trellis
where she sits and sorts
swarm the domestic atrocities.

Again and again she tells
their names and their names
do not control them...

This sweetness is almost
unendurable. With her pale
wrist she dabs at her eyes;
unheard, the perfect drops
patter into the kitchen chalice.

THE GUARDIAN TREE

Unlike that manor oak
in Northamptonshire
it did not climb within our walls,
right-angle with the roofbeam,
and overhead explode
into a flurry of leaves.
Out in Iceland
on the howling farmsteads
solitary trees graze outer walls,
they lean against each other
in mutual dependence.
It was not like these.

No dragon gnawing at its root,
no eagle in its high uneasy branches,
no deer, no goats
tearing at the green shoots:
nothing fabulous or universal.
No fructifer, no seductive
sweet dew on its leaves,
no spirit-ladder.

We seldom gave it thought:
a guess at its age
and surprise it survived a bomb
meant for the Docks;
a second desultory guess
(being neither children nor trigonometrists)
at its huge reaching height;
though we fretted at its red scab, and peered
for the lost canary,
and raked and cursed and
carted off its leaves,
and once, one June evening,
we made love beneath it,
inviolate
as its green arms
waved away the world.

Not only bereft now;
abandoned, as children by a mother.
It was our cap of happiness,
rough-tongued and embracing,
our pennyplain guardian tree,
rooted in earth but
free of doubt and cause and argument,
rising above change.

ORKNEY GIRLS: THE GIRL AT GURNESS

I become little more than a voice:
a bruck of bones earth-fingered,
all unravelled and unlimbed
by salts and seep and vapours.

There! The whale-path to a farm
on a fiord, a girl in sunlight;
that road to the Irishman, clover
on his tongue, and the whirlpool of love,
and that is the way of the dove
to Jorsala. I have no knowledge
of where that way leads my brothers
with blooming axe and scramasax.

I am only in shadow saying,
Look at the rib of water passing –
the show of aquamarine, limpid,
and the lumpen everyday swell,
the furious spears of black-and-silver;
saying, Look at the shift of light
gilding the bare breasts of Rousay.

The wind is a wearisome impartial
scold. Think of the ways you also
took, or did not take…

(Mouth stopped. Two shoulder brooches.
An iron knife. Also lobster-shell,
an unbroken necklace, blushing pink-and-lilac.)

PREPARATORY SCHOOL

Licker Lonsdale could tap dance.
His hot eyes stripped us
naked so Murdoch the Mole used to burrow
beneath his blankets before
lights out.

Unlike Henry's generous backhanders
(purple stripes on the badge of the buttocks),
Grummet's half-nelsons brought me to my knees.

Holland had some pox and was nicknamed Morbus.
He left the term before I came;
thus I was accorded his name.

Hymn 25 in the *Public School Hymnbook.*
The day thou gavest, Lord,
the one day between now and half-term.
My tears lolloped on to the page.

Coronation Week, Sunday sweet shop,
lashing Henry's horrible daughter
to the crumbling Wellingtonia...

And up the usual decrepit drive,
past mature trees
and the scoreboard showing the whole team
out for 13,

I listen to the silence of your preparation
for the mad dash
past the vultrine crucifix
into the gloom,

then angrily reason with myself
all the way from Otford west into Dorset
watching your reflection
in the mirror
dissolve.

HAPPY BIRTHDAY

for Dominic at 16

How do you do, bone-house?
Here's another stepping-stone
on this risky journey –
another pause for understandings:

three pawns are worth more
than a bishop: the more I give,
the more I have to give;
no perspective without humour;

panache wins admirers; to act,
always to be my own audience;
language ties and language cuts,
mightier than Excalibur.

You will bother to read this
and take issue with it
one way or another
almost as a matter of principle.

You have a sort of spiky grace,
like a conker in its armour,
a crocketed spire, the elbows
and knees of the contrary sea.

Happy birthday, bone-house!
Here's another stepping-stone
on this risky journey –
another pause for understandings:

remember the child I'm leaving;
work against small wars;
today colours tomorrow; I will
not miss the boat to the stars.

ANGELS AT ST MARY'S

'The angels have gone'
Church Guide, Walsham-le-Willows

Up among bleached stars and suns
Are the tongues, protruding, oak pegs
Wanting their smiling high-fliers.

The fledglings heard black hints
And saw battle-lights advancing.
They conferred, they spread their wings.

Or did they become spirits of
Themselves? Angels rearranged,
Acute angles where clear sound and

Sunlight cross? They are in the air.

ON THE WAY EAST

The terminus smells of wild garlic,
The buttoned cloth is squirrel red-brown.
There are depths as black as black holes
Where the barley has been beaten down.

The caparisoned elms are alight
(Each stilled in a flood of gold fire).
Such dawdles! Standstills! The white
Skyline is lanced by a crocketed spire.

Wild roses cling to pink brick. The track
Is burning sienna. Almost, almost free!
Beyond the hectares of mangel and beet
Open silver-grey arms, stunning, the sea.

COMFORT

Who said anything about comfort?
Those syllables do not rhyme
with zinc slakes or ice-bright sky.
The sea is grinding her spears.
Up creeks and gullies, over groynes
the black tide surges
and the hag wind rides her.
In the bleak forest on the staithe
rigging clacks and chitters.

Little but memory for company,
wild geese, swans whooping,
but no urbanity no
gossip prejudice bitterness sham.
In London I dream of these harsh folds,
the sea's slam, the light's eagle eye,
and here again I draw
this place – hair-shirt, dear cloak –
around such infirmities.

The Painting-Room (1988)

from **THE PAINTING-ROOM**

Creatures of a Landscape

The truant with his rod,
and cap on the back of his head;
the apple-face on the passing lighter;
and the lad astride the carthorse,
yoked to his destiny:

I'm looking at
the creatures of a paradise garden
they will never leave entirely.

How little will happen
in the whole span of their lives
not already present and planted.
They're almost fixed!

For them as for you and me
the ethic of work
will not be a matter of choice
or self-discovery
but almost an inheritance:
a fierce imperative decreed over their cradles
by a stern godmother.

And when we believe
that whatsoever we do or say
has moral implications,
it's only what our parents told us
and we observe each day
in the order of this land around us.

This dear, familiar, unshowy Eden!
It's the child of history.
It feeds me and I'll nourish it.

The Language of Light

I rise with the rising bell
every day of the week.
The river is my pointer
to read the landscape's book.

I'll sit and watch these willow
leaves silvered by the wind
until they are impressed
on the cool page of my mind.

And then these twisted roots
dressed with wads of sponge:
I'll watch them in this calm sun
until the shadows change.

I'll live in these meadows
and trace each variant.
It's with their light they speak
the language of the heart.

Correspondences

That's her!
So well disposed to the world:
the gaze unstopped, the kind shoulder.

But on my way here
I saw her in the cornfield:
her carriage, her smouldering mane.
She was gathering with the gleaners.

And that grave girl by the porch:
when I heard her,
soft and foggy
as a flute at the bottom of its register,
I thought for a moment…

She surprises me
everywhere
and I say to myself
there is no time when I have not loved her.

I can hear my own voice.
Not proving signs or symbols
but correspondences
are what I am looking for.
As I walk with the river
and hear, or think I hear,
the far, late harvest bell,
I see her
in the sweet incline of this willow,
the moist leaves. The dry whispers
of the flags are like a Greek chorus.

And here, this torso, aching and arched...

Ox-bow and lock and race:
there's laughter in the water
and salt in her veins...

That's her!
Did you see her
invested
and trailing green-and-gold chains?

    Like Light that Gilds

She loves me and her love is light
like light that gilds the river's braid
when water-meadows drown in shade
and Bergholt's wrapped in rings of night.

Her guardians check, forbid and blight
and still her colours do not fade.
She loves me and her love is light
like light that gilds the river's braid.

Do they believe she has no fight?
Or think our love can be betrayed?
Shining, constant and unafraid,
she guides my hand and gilds my sight

like light that gilds the river's braid.

Quiet and Unquiet

In the lap of water
and the company of watermen:

the boatwright with peaceful hands
building the lighter
that will lift with the lock
the keeper is turning;
and the poler, all purpose and clout,
about to yell
at the fisherman dibbling for nothing much.

There is something
similar about these well-tempered men:
their calm brows and their bearing
and every line of their bodies
announce a complete want of anxiety.

As if to advertise the manual life,
or to say
the rod assuages,
or to commend the properties of water.

When I grow quiet,
and ready myself, and start to write,
I am one
of this engaged and placid company.

It's off the page and outside the frame
my mind snags.

Errant son, or telephone silent,
time short and money short:
the shadows lengthen,
everywhere the causes of indisposition.
It was the same for you.

Fisher was right:
worry hurts the stomach more than arsenic.
It soon generates nothing but itself.

And yet to celebrate
this company of watermen
at their usual stations, calm and accepting...

I think we would agree
the presence of unquiet
quite essential,
vital as yeast.

   Oak Leaf

This little gossip, silly
and still crumpled, tender
as a tongue! This lobe's twice
pierced, this mole almost amber...
       this one and this one

I picked it from the sapling
you planted at the gate,
now ample as a cumulus
childbearing and forthright
       this one and this one
       and the world is wide

No two hours are alike
and no two leaves on a tree.
Let me learn the singular
green lessons of the eye
       this one and this one
       and the world is wide
       this one and only

   In Pursuit

Under rookwings
and the tatty crown,
under the lanes of clouds,
dove and lily and oyster in the dome,
the labours of the months proceed:

the ferryman and his mate
and the blinkered white horse in harness,

the plough, the little boat
with its nose in shadow, its oars
at this moment shipped,

all part of the same arduous story
the water reflects
and invigorates.

Observation close and continual…
to realize, not to feign…
less to inspire than inform…
and this pursuit
not to be looked on with blind wonder
but legitimate, scientific and mechanical.

I understand this too:
matter is deadweight
and form nothing but a shape
the breath of life makes beautiful.
Lightness and brightness.
The tint of English daylight, cool.

When Chantrey took your palette
and scumbled the whole foreground
with smears of asphaltum:
'There goes all my dew.'

In My Painting-Room

Wherever I step wherever I look
the canvas-weave is covered in blossom,
impasted with chestnut, cherry and lilac,

Queen Anne's lace and ropes of laburnum.
My galloping boys spring out of the brush;
and my girls, all gingham and sweet alyssum,

skip past the millrace's passion-and-rush;
and now my wife glances up at our home –
I'll dress her in sunlight: a loop of gold wash.

Child-willow, cloud-woman, the river's in bloom:
surge and reflection – life, resurrection –
lift their bright voices in my painting-room

SOUNDS

for my father on his seventieth birthday

You dug the chalky soil; we blazed spring-trails
through high, sopping beechwoods; and in the shed
examined, catalogued and then displayed
quartz crystals, coins, potsherds from Bledlow Ridge,
fossils from the chalk-pit; at night I heard
you play – while you charmed babeldom I slept.

After a while I brought you drafts. I thought
the gardener and walker-in-the-rain,
the patient keeper with whom once I found
a Constantine, the music-man whose Dance
was sung in mildewed church, cathedral nave
and concert hall would know about word-spells.

You treated them with proper seriousness.
I see you at your study door, smiling,
taking the sheets; and then you close your eyes,
withdraw into that magic gloom of books,
piano, harmonisphere, preparing for
our sessions with small signs and spider-marks.

You thinned my words like seedlings. *And avoid*
long words where short suffice. (Work; will do.)
For vogue and buzz and all-too-commonplace
you wrote in almost timeless substitutes
(ex-Yeats, ex-Graves). *Revise and then revise.*
Our second thoughts strike deeper than the first.

Sometimes you mused aloud, or asked me how
my craft related to the science of sound –
abstract in this, its power akin to music.
And sound, you told me then, *includes silence.*
One part of the performance, integral…
I hear myself. Hear all that's left unsaid.

NAMING YOU

We have not snared you
with the net of a name
we have not tamed you

you are energy the one
word that is every word
the sound of the gong

come into the garden
we will sing you
white stars green leaves

such spring-fever
the birds hop and cheep
around your sleepy head

the surge and shining
the rocking of tall trees
in the eager wind

who are you what are you
but the little sister
of this world around you

morning star and sparrow
bluebell smouldering
the attentive yew

*

but the dance of time
the argument of choice
fingers reach out

well the world can wait
we are disciples
and nothing is arbitrary

you are your own word
and cannot grow out of
a careless visitation

you declare yourself
smiling bubble-blower
your eyes gentian blue

lolling by the willow
your bald head askew
like a medieval saint
come home little sister
take your proper place
in this shining garden

dear daughter come home
come home we are here
and listening for your name

OENONE IN JANUARY

January 1st: Beginning

Fingers chapped, the clean year picked and scraped
to a glint. Halley's Comet a milk burr.
Over the long field silhouettes, guffaws,
resolutions. Then the boisterous wind.

January 2nd: Ages

She carts, cherishes and upbraids her dolls,
sowing the seeds of her own motherhood.
She is every age already. You look
as she sleeps: creaseless ancient Infanta.

January 3rd: Pretence

You core it and she eats the skin, the flesh
and then the hole! When she covers her eyes
she is hidden. She deceives you with pearls.
You hear her laughter in the swollen stream.

January 4th: Taming

Buttons, clips, pins – she always takes her tithe.
She drills tins and bottles. Nothing counter
passes without some question or comment.
This fierce attempt on the unwieldy world!

January 5th: Absences

Not maybes – those tassels whiskers, that lump
in the mattress tigerish – but maybe nots:
Can't see them! Can't hear them! Am I alone?
Bawling existentialist before dawn.

January 6th: Animateur

Spangles on her pane. Icicles wrist thick,
thick as ropes and candid. Dark clots knitted
up in the elms. The whole frieze in need of
its animateur. She opens one eye.

January 7th: Imagining

You smile, murmur mouse, think she clambers up
to share one pillow and rehearse the day...
Gulls circle mewing. You turn to the clock,
and it's not even time for her to wake.

January 8th: Invocation

All morning the sleet slanted in. She stripped
to the waist and donned seven necklaces.
Doily, felt-tips (heavy duty): she raised
a rose garden and entered it, singing.

January 9th: Numbers

One more, no more... In her reckoning, what
is ever complete? *Where has he went?*
It's a shame they can't come both. I am three
years old; when will I be all the numbers?

January 10th: Hair

A thousand clefs of curls. Her mother laughs
and says corn-gold (her own is titian).
Bright cloud, you think; grace notes of the skylark,
ocean, elixir... *Nope*, she says. *Ginger!*

January 11th: Half-Brother

She knows it's almost time for him to go.
Silver chatterbox, she trots at his heels,

dragoons him into last loud games. He smiles,
devoted, tolerant; a kind of god.

January 12th:Recognition

Good morning path! Oh! good morning puddle!
Blithe bubble all the way to Sunday School.
St Francis' sister, greeting one and all
as newborn and equal and integral.

January 13th: Rites

She takes your lobes between fingers and thumbs,
gently massages; rubs noses; warbles
into one ear. Close your eyes. Celebrate
the siren rites of the true Daughterhood!

January 14th: Rivals

Each used to undivided attention;
each queering the other's pitch. Carnations
blaze in the razor sunlight. Two *divas*
(old and young) glaring across their breakfasts!

January 15th: Chastening

That weal on the back of her hand your hand
inflicted, and the doleful cutting tears,
part sting, part shock, and part calculation:
you know it was right and feel quite stricken.

January 16th: Nightsounds

Uhu of the barn owl; cock pheasant's creak;
hackle and cackle; our lyric willow;
and always this ancient house, its whispers
and predictions. One listener: her heart.

January 17th: Dangers

That tinny sound as she tries out thin ice!
In its shine you see capsizes, crashes,
every kind of accident, then, far worse,
the smiling drivers… Take steps. And take steps.

January 18th: Joy

Lily, she thought; she thought, *tiger. And this
is my own daughter: dayspring and dancer
and gleam.* The late primrose light faded from
the little room. Still she looked; still she shone.

January 19th: Mother!

The least knock or scratch or ache and you are
supernumerary. Back to the source:
mā-tr, mē-tē-r, mō-dor, mutter, máthair…
She cries and reaches out. The woman smiles.

January 20th: Dog

Beau Brummel and Barnum and Loyal Sam!
He's her chief barker and mooning paleface,
her game opponent, grinning accomplice.
She tightens the leash: *Jealous! You're jealous!*

January 21st: Imitation

Wading round the room in black stilettos;
intent, loading a pipette; kneading dough,
sleeves rolled up: flatterer in rehearsal,
instinct with longing to learn, to succeed.

January 22nd: Lexicon

*Why not can't I do it? Of course I can.
Slobber-de-bob! Isgusting! There's water*

in frogtime. I want to read peoplest books.
I'll run you down. What colour is your talk?

January 23rd: Sunrise

You left both ladies in the pink, fingertips
at their temples. Each stone and each leaf
was locked in bristling frost; the whole circuit
of the sky down-pillows and pear-blossom.

January 24th: Rules

Playing percentage is unknown to her.
Draws you wide, kicks the chalk, always ends up
in dock and nettles. Proper anarchist,
years of markings stretched out in front of her.

January 25th: Spring?

Sunlight. Hedgerows and high-wavers all stripped,
all winter-bleached and ready to begin.
The dog waltzes over the fields. She primes
her shining pots with earth and warm gravel.

January 26th: Promises

Her rainbow segments dance; her cardboard clock
with its bold promise pulses. Poor sleeper,
turn, twitch, and twist, whisper of Horrid things.
Slowly her dove unfurls morning-white wings.

January 27th: Offenders

Her sequinned, squinting elephant exiled
on the landing is the offending book
your devoted grandmother blue-pencilled
and filleted. Each day it grows larger.

January 28th: Proposals

Hot and hectic and armed with a posse
of proposals: *pick-stickers; picklecheese;
house-of-cards; Humpty; stand-on-my-head...*
You, niggard, had one and only one: *bed!*

January 29th: There

There it snows. Here it always rains quiet always-rain
dropping into your skull. And there the north
and east winds blow. Here the colours hang limp.
There the rose. Here – how sharply you miss her.

January 30th: Commitment

Hide your eyes! She tears across the room, throws
herself on to the Chesterfield, face down,
enters a white shining darkness: no game,
no commitment ever more serious.

January 31st: Goodbye

The world is opening under our feet;
you stoop, sweep her up, you kiss her goodbye.
Three and already a breaker of hearts:
I won't see you ever again, will I?

CORNUCOPIA

for Gillian

Globe

You cradle the globe in your cupped hands.
It is flawed and freckled, and will weep
if you bite it. Circle of dark secrets.

Sustenance

Tawny oats and barley, sinful couch-grass:
the sultry compass nods as you settle
and smile and bare your golden breast.

Plenitude

Orchard of the body, body of the corn,
and in your complete and fourfold garden
moon-faced onions hang on the flaking wall,
wasps crawl over the last of the clover,
the black mulberries hang heavy with blood,
and a buck hare stares at his reflection.

Intentions

In your bright room you brandish a sheaf
of intentions. You're lifting this old house,
with its grey ruff of doves, and shaking it
by the scruff. But in this wink-and-glint
our discussions are decorous as games
of chess. I move caution; I move cash.
Your moves are never only all they seem,
and now you are so many moves ahead.

On Balance

This day belongs to your elder daughter.
Between wild strawberries so late they will

not ripen, and your crumpled pink roses,
she pedalled and balanced for the first time,
not yet four. I saw your grimace and grin –
that fierce unique desire for each of our
children not only to excel but excel us.
I should say this day belongs to you.

Colours

You wear russet and mole and olive;
less often, amber, umber, vermilion.
Yours are the colours of fruition and earth.
Nothing wan or obvious or irresolute.

Here and Now

Little time for the colour of tomorrow,
even less for the cloud of unknowing:
you build your house on the cornerstone
of Now and view with an indifferent eye
the whole condition of uncertainty.

Ledger

But at the equinox you look over your
shoulder. When days mist and the scales tip,
you pull down and dust your faded ledger
and inscribe lances of sunlight (your own
family's occasions) in phrases rapid
and rosy as the leaves on the wild vine.

Toll

Sepulchral clouds and scudding days: your
head's on my shoulder in the lee of the dune,
half-guarded from the wind and whip-and-spike
of the marram. Over the pale strand
the bourdon tolls. The air mauves and quivers.

Studio

A seventh wave, you galleon in and
redistribute everything: flotsam and jetsam
beached by the last tide, already bleached
and curling; the regular bed of nondescripts;
and not concealed but simply overwhelmed,
the precious shapes you're working on,
shining and bold, crucial as blood.
What abundance! So profuse you cannot
be contained, drawing and redrawing lines,
you draw us all into your one design.

Woman

Tap-root; all eyes, breasts and stomach.
Your body's wave breaking, salt and honey.
Sanctus, the angels sing, sanctus, sanctus.
Peace-weaver, pillow-talker, raising this old house.
My five-pointed star, my point of
departure and return.

DO YOU, OR I, OR ANYONE KNOW?

It comes up by the roots
                              dangling and unfortunate,
a straggler and victim on the field's margin
never quite caught up in the bruised gold tides.

The air's an intoxicant, laced with the sweetness
of the barley, and clay, and far thunder.

You shake off the chaplet of storm-flies
and, sharp as a bright stoat, bite through
the hempen stalk.
                              You're holding a wand.
A lick of lightning…
                              You break off one grain
and tickle it round the cradle of your palm.
It's a kingdom! First you peel away
pale-striped bullseye skin, then plain wrapping.

And now, half-a-minute later, the dark sky-growl.
The storm's still half-a-county off!
                              The smiling cleft;
the ivory sheen; the warm grain still malleable.

You grind it and grit it. Unconvinced
of its relationship to barley-water, you spit it out.

Now the beard: one whisker. You hold the hilt
and run it smoothly between your fingers.
You rub it the wrong way and say, 'It's biting!'

Nothing the eye can see,
                              unlike the storm
gathering and sending shivers through the barley.
Later, you lift my little brass microscope
from its wooden box.
                              How you surprise my childhood!
Properly ginger, you lay the whisker on the glass tray.

I light a kitchen candle – rain-spears and thunder
drive in through the garden gate –
and fiddle with the mirror, the tube, the mirror…

Barba dentata: covering one eye with soft fingertips
you level your unblinking gaze.

HERE, AT THE TIDE'S TURNING

You close your eyes and see
                    the stillness of
the mullet-nibbled arteries, samphire
on the mudflats almost underwater,
and on the saltmarsh whiskers of couch-grass
twitching, waders roosting, sea-lavender
faded to ashes.

                    In the dark or almost dark
shapes sit on the staithe muttering of plickplack,
and greenshanks, and zos beds;

            a duck arrives
in a flap, late for a small pond party.

The small yard's creak and groan and lazy rap,
muffled water music.

                One sky-streamer,
pale and half-frayed, still dreaming of colour.

Water and earth and air quite integral:
all Waterslain one sombre aquarelle.

From the beginning, and last year, this year,
you can think of no year when you have
not sat on this stub of a salt-eaten stanchion.

Dumbfounded by such tracts of marsh and sky –
the void swirled round you and pressed against you –
you've found a mercy in small stones.

This year, next year, you cannot think
of not returning: not to perch in the blue
hour on this blunt jetty, not to wait, as of right,
for the iron hour and the turning of the tide.

You cross the shillying and the shallows
and, stepping on to the marsh, enter
a wilderness.

Quick wind works around you.

You are engulfed in a wave of blue flames.

No line that is not clear cut and severe,
nothing baroque or bogus. The voices
of young children rehearsing on the staithe
are lifted from another time.

This is
battleground. Dark tide fills the winking pulks,
floods the mud-canyons.

This flux, this anchorage.

Here you watch, you write, you tell the tides.
You walk clean into the possible.

PORLOCK: INTERRUPTED LIVES

Amongst these pink and grey stones,
some smooth, some dressed with ocean runes,
eleven US airmen died;
the salt has almost eaten their names.

The little copper plaque, crammed
by some loving inexperienced hand
(ten men identified and one unknown)
is no longer fastened
tight to the ashen headstone,

and quite soon the stone itself
will crack, or topple
and fall, and for several months
no one will even notice.

A pony down from the moors
nuzzles it; the glistening spoor
of a snail bandages it...

Nearby I see what might have been
a little shore sanctuary – a place for prayer
or else a pen for black-faced sheep –
reduced to an oblong shape,
almost no more than a shadow
amongst these dry, quite cordial stones.

I see a mound
and lumps not readily to be explained,
then all around the signs
of other lives and other times.

And where this wilderness is almost bald
I find doomed spears
of samphire irrupting and withering
and a single ragged thistle –
a purple perch
for a butterfly with clouded yellow wings;

and led on by the piping
of a small bird I cannot even see,
come upon a clump of quivering bleached campion.

I stoop and count
the white and shining petals –
ten and eleven and eleven and eleven.

THE SIGNS OF WALSHAM

I have seen the way in. Rightangles and rubber swerves
and deep scummy ditches. I have seen the puzzle on the
palimpsest: the forest of elm and ash, the watering
places.

I have seen the green women, all very elegant, very
particular, trilling in forever light painted in tempera.

I have seen matriarchs who buried their husbands. The
rectitude of pit-props; last survivors. Dispensers of
pullets' eggs and grace-and-favour houses.

Also the old snorters, beady, broad and blunt. I have
seen their terrible horizons.

A woman drifted, she died while spring skipped outside
her window. A newborn baby lolled in the shadow
of the yew tree. I have seen them.

I have seen tides: exiles from collapses and sagging
thatches, shoals of children, the lissom baby-sitters.
Also the old soaks, looking meaningful; buzzing
weekenders; nasal upstarts aspiring to jacuzzis.

I have seen the crusader who lost his name his date and
the crant for poor Mary who lost her heart and died. I
have seen the tradesmen hiding in the wall, the leftover
smiles of oak angels.

I have seen lists of sponsors and meringue-makers,
paragraphs of small type concerning covenants.

Every eighth minute the Bangalore Bomber. The light
plane stoops with its deadly spray. The F1-11s set out
for Libya. I have seen them.

I have seen the kestrel and the tree-creeper; the
sun-splash butterflies; the blue sheen on a dragonfly's
wings.

The circle of smiles ringing the pink cottages; I have
seen it. I have seen slight shoulders, stooping shoulders
sharing heavy weather.

Change-ringers stand in the tower. Clay throws up
gold. I have seen layer upon layer. And every day this
jackwind and its small rearrangements.

ABOVE THE SPRING LINE

in celebration of the Ridgeway

1

Under the moon's pale razor
under the warm eye
under the chamber of clouds
under rain-dance and hail-bounce

in this latitude of shadows

blazing the green limbs
foot-friend and far-reacher
master of compounds

2

Overseer of Epona and the fleet horses at Lambourn
the bigwigs in their hill-stations at Silbury and Chequers

keeper of Dragon Hill and the craters on the bombing range
also the quaking grass the brome grass melilot and eyebright

warden of the Og and the watercress beds and Goring Gap
the sarsens like dowdy sheep and the dowdy sheep like sarsens

custodian of the downs and brakes the strip lynchets and warrens
under the lapwing the glider's wing spring of yellow-hammers

3

And spring is the word. I can almost forget
yesterday – the sweat stain semen stain smudge
of chalk and in the hedge the sodden butts
the jagged bottle and a bloodstained rag

Here are wiry snowdrops bedded in beech mast
where wild pigs rooted. Fuses everywhere
The spindle and bryony shrug their shoulders
Birch-twigs pinken, generations within

4

A man laps at a dewpond, lays his hoar-head on his knapsack
knobby with Brandon flint. A girl in a mauve shift bares her throat
Trials riders tight-lipped burn through crimson and purple rosettes

A crocodile of the literal-minded steamy and singing
I will lift up mine eyes set their sights on the escarpment
Ah! the drover sleeps in a butterfly wimple – chalk-hill blues
flutter in and out of his mouth and here above the spring line
a hunter smiles as he snares such a pretty Chiltern gentian

5

It is all within me
written in chalk, and written
in your hand it is yours

Whatever you may also choose...

From Overton and Ivinghoe
Sunlight and ribs of shadow
pressing behind us and coursing
through us. We are conductors

New & Selected Poems (1991)

SPEAKING OF THE SNOW

1 Prism

I can see a lily spathe
and something like a moon-dog
and the globe of a tear.
Turn this face to face you
and it all becomes clear.
This world is light and what
is impossible? You may think
for one moment you have
trapped a dancing star.

2 Snowman

The old coal-and carrot
routine! A wrap around my neck;
perhaps the cap of consolation.
But when all's done so damned
provisional, the work of
innocents eager to reshape
this world in their own image.
They're mainly water themselves,
and do not even know it.

3 Lover

I could write burning softness.
Or blinding plumage. Or fleece.
Remember Dafydd ap Gwilym:
The spume of fighting dragons.
But fleece comes nearest...
I could also simply say
you cover everything. The way
I see you there is nothing
that is not touched by you.

4 Old Man

The bright birds return to us
something of ourselves. Babies
burble, children greet them
stamping and shouting.
I watch them spin and weave,
though; I see their feathers
are frozen. In my skin
I wait, often turning
back towards the children.

5 He Who Hesitates

Tonight, how can I reach her?
Will I ever hear her voice
and speak to her again? Flecked
with silver: will I touch her skin?
I want her; do I want her?
This is a cage of questions.
And now? Have I already left
leaving too late? Once it starts
to snow, does it ever stop?

6 Prisoner

Stumps and boles and dark eyes!
There's glitter in the air,
faces at frost-windows trying
to be brave, unable to be brave.
What were the questions never
put and the words not spoken?
Walkers and skiers stream
past, noiseless, and under
the ice dead children swim.

7 The Fair Field

A broken army of stick-people
stumbled out of le Brocquy,
exiles on their own patch,
genderless, ageless, all of them
stiff-legged, darkened by distance.
I saw some had been weeping.
How the fair field winked and shone.
Each one, I wrote, leaned
forward with a long way to go.

BLUE WINGS

Something bright and blue and flying...

Yesterday a man I know,
with perfect sight,
not given to hyperbole or legpulling,
spotted a mountain-lion.

Here!
So far north and east,
after so long!

Old countrymen
ask what size
and when and where
and whether sky-blue, gun-barrel, cornflower.

They pronounce
dragonfly,
then bluebird, humming-bird, bat

and one man is doubtless right

as I who say
                for a moment
I saw in flight
the blue wings of what's possible.

SOLVITUR AMBULANDO

Left the log house with a weight on my back:
the old world, the whole world, slung in a sack
that rocked me from side to side. Couldn't stop
thinking, stop think-thinking, muttering shop
for a mile or so down the shining track.

Large as a flittermouse a butterfly
steered past me, steered and waved, sailed on the dry
thyme-rich ocean. Stepped over a beetle,
an aged scarab hammered from metal
emerald and black. The how, when and why

never bothered them. They followed their bliss.
Watched a zebra caterpillar, careless
of the rapids, a dirt-track rider,
scramble to the verge where a scarlet spider,
nothing but instinct, scaled a wild iris.

Must think, must think-think. Every inch counts...
But look at the hill-horse, its whisk-and-flounce!
Played seek and hide and seek with a quickstick
cardinal; rerouted a thirsty tick;
the sack began to lighten, ounce by ounce.

Tilted my hat, down on all fours, stalking:
Two deer high-tailed it, swerving and forking
and criss-crossing.
                  Fireflies danced all that night.
On one wrist I wore a bracelet of light.
I dreamed the old dream: solve it by walking.

ACROSS THE WATER

In the end he did not leave us
but we rowed away downstream.
My little daughter crouched in the stern
and kept on asking. All day was dark
but that was when the clouds began
to separate, and the late sunlight
singled him out. Over the immense
purple tide we saw him leaning back
and staring up, his neck shining.
He could not hear us calling out
across the water, and my daughter stood
up. Each time we waved he waved.

GENERATIONS OF AIR

I was the bellows boy. And in corners
decorated with curious tidemarks
or up against grey walls frosted with salts
I pumped and the monsters with twenty throats
or forty throats shuddered and wheezed.

Then the old sorcerer showed them his palms
and soles: they hooted and began to sing.
The last words he said to me (pulling out
from under the bedclothes not a green note
for me and a brown note for my sister,
as was customary, but his own right hand,
mottled and weedy, which he inspected
and arpeggioed across the scarlet):
That noble beast at Creake: feed him sometimes!

But in these frantic days, a mere ten years
before the millennium, most of
the menagerie is under lock and key.
The keepers no longer trust the visitors
who carry crow-bars in their handbags,
and snaffle the plate, and either cannot see
or cannot tolerate the beautiful.
And then, despite the mighty efforts

of Mrs Carwithen, and that chronicle
of practice culminating on the day
of the Coronation, my reading's poor
and I'm a poor interpreter, sounding out
the cadences of foreign tongue
I still won't resign myself to not learning.

South Creake was open, though. I stood once more
under the amused, expectant angels,
marvelling at the bourdon, the cornopean
and the oboe d'amour, and it seemed to me
the old man taught me neither team spirit
nor love of music (I honour my mother,
I honour my father) but how to listen.

Here for instance, close to Creake, in the village
where he died, beneath the raucous gulls
fishing and flying on errands, white on pearl,
I listen to the suck and drag of the creek
returning to its source, and the source
itself no more than a tremor, the sense
you are not listening to silence.

Not only to listen but to hear
myself, and come to read the signs.
To man the machine! This is what I learned –
grandfather, this and the virtues
of discipline. Always to keep steady;
to keep the beat with my left hand.
To draw deep lungfuls. Generations of air.

BLUE OF BLUE

Wild grapes!
          My fingertips are blue
and I'm alert,
cockahoop as a Viking!

Half this arboretum's blue,
                    or blue.
I've tracked every page
searching for the value.

Not this jay,
            screaming obscenities,
this pair of pygmy blues;
neither the smalt eye
            of the iris
nor the needles of the spruce, and
certainly not
            this blatant turquoise bug.

But I'm on target!
This is the register,

somewhere
          in here
I've seen another blue,
                  more elusive
– feathered cloud, simmering,
neck of smoke
            with a blue fume
– I could have sworn it.

No racket!
          Every movement passionate,
          every word painful.
Siberian eyes.
          Somewhere in here
                    this unerring

blue of blue
with no name
      until I name it:
my fingertips are blue
          and I mean
to entertain it.

The Language of Yes (1996)

THE LANGUAGE OF YES

This world's wreckers are at their games
and everywhere it is late.

Words words words a fury of words
hype and shred and prate,
sanitise, speculate;
they please themselves.

How can I be content
with hollow professions
or the arm's length of the sceptic?
Even with the sensory,
the pig heart's slop-and-mess?

I still want.

Let me make and remake the word
which reveals itself,
unexpected, always various,

and be so curious
(affirmation's mainspring)
I sing the language of yes.

ELEANOR'S ADVENT

Mother's Song for the First Sunday

Which came first: word or dream?
Silver shiver on a screen,
I prayed for you and you were born.

Dumpling dancing in my womb.
Long-armed, long-legged, little frog.
I prayed for you and you were born

and I am born a second time,
my saving child-of-Bethlehem.
You are my offering; my gift;
still my loving perfect stranger.

Let me light your first candle.

December 3rd

Condensation, freezing fog, English blur.
Smoky December, that's what Martial says.
She heard a blackbird sing, and saw it surf-and-
splash out of blazing pyracantha.

December 4th

She instals herself, draped in her duvet
or her winking cat. She inserts her thumb
and her presence settles us. Four-year-old
omphalos, the world spinning around her.

December 5th

How this story fascinates her! But what
if it should change? What if the wolf escapes
next time? She will not take her eyes off it
and asks me to read it again. Again.

December 6th

Some are fruit, some flowers: her sister is
long-fingered fern, maybe water-lily.
But she's a compote – no, a macédoine:
mulberry and plum, mango, persimmon.

December 7th

Her mother's speckled kimono: it's like,
she announces, and falters, wordfishing:
like bubbles what frogs make. Then they grow up.
They all change into gorgeous butterflies.

December 8th

Seeing how we hurt ourselves, and hurt each
other, she neither quails nor questions why.
Wheresoever there's a wound, she bustles
forward, shining, and plants a flower in it.

Sister's Song for the Second Sunday

Miss Eleanor Edith Sarah:
she's horrible, my sister.

On walks she whines all the way:
my path my dog my one my my...
She makes you say, 'scuse me 'scuse me,
and takes my toys to annoy me,

especially my doll. She always
wants to wear a dress, even on days

when there's ice. If I could teach her
to be good, I would for sure.

Let me light your second candle.

December 10th

First snowflakes and she snubs her nose against
the glass. Light. Wet. I say it won't settle.
In lieu of last year's mighty snow-woman,
she suggests we try for a snow-baby.

December 11th

Mother: I heard you reading to yourself.
Ellie: Yes, and I'm learning to read now.
Mother: That's good. Your teacher will be pleased.
Ellie: Don't be silly! She can read too.

December 12th

Ελένη: bright one, river eyes shining
and a comedian's long upper lip.
Lullay my liking, Eleanor sweeting,
traipser and trooper, my small lollipop.

December 13th

There is a third – her little sister – and
sometimes she cries out, always beginning,
never getting anywhere. At midnight
my lost wife sweeps from room to empty room.

December 14th

Why is Christmas, daddy? So I tell her
the good tidings: silly shepherds, wise men,
a star, a stable. And Christmas, I say,
is Jesus's birthday. Don't say Jesus!

December 15th

A damnation of rooks, and sky so pale
blue it looks almost breakable. There's rime
on the lawn, each blade bristling, delicate:
a dazzling page she writes on, step by step.

Father's Song for the Third Sunday

I saw your first breath, breathless.
On my palms I weighed you, weightless.
Your lying so defenceless armed me.
Hearing your first scream, I sang.

In England white with ropes of blossom,
or in December, in Judæa.
Like Joseph the carpenter.
Like any father, anywhere,

crying *my daughter, my daughter,*
ich freue mich in dir.

Let me light your third candle.

December 17th

Spillikins, Memory, and jigsaw race:
she wants it understood she'll win. And when
she does, intent and pink, rosebud mouth pursed,
her first thought is to console the losers.

December 18th

Today her red-gold sister is not here,
so she controls the air-space, costume-chest,
felt-tips, VCR. She pulls out her thumb!
Easy sunlight and she sails into speech.

December 19th

As she looks, she is: Baroque puttela
not to be misled or lightly shaken.
Little redeemer! We nearly called her
Rosamund. We could have called her Petra.

December 20th

More ribbon, more lace, more leaping colour:
ambassadress from the courts of summer,
wearing ripe cherries; wearing whole borders!
Gardens, she says, are never quite cloudy.

December 21st

Long-lost, new-found: carolling to herself,
she claims her first brother. Locks on to him
like a limpet. And sitting in his lap,
arms about his neck, wins him for ever.

December 22nd

Sickly-sweet cloud around the sugarbeet
factory; jaundiced sun; and a songthrush
plump on the path, eyes fixed on kingdom come:
the most beautiful bird in the whole world.

Eleanor's Song for the Fourth Sunday

I saw a shooting star tonight.
   Christmas in the air!
And Jesus's birthday is tomorrow
   – what dress can I wear?
I'll sing, I'll kiss him when he cries,
   I'll brush his baby hair;
I'll bake him a birthday cake,
   and teach him a prayer.
I'll say thank you for having me.
   But... will he be there?

Let me light your fourth candle.

December 24th

Her quiet diligence is motherly,
her devotion Marian: unaware
she is aware of the power of love
entire. Amor! Quam dulcis est amor!

Envoi

And so she springs her box of days: hours past
and time to come. Jack Frost gnaws at the panes
but in her room a peacock stirs, flutters
to the Christmas light: momentary and sweet.

STILL LIFE: ELEANOR WITH FIELD-FLOWERS

At last the bones. After
the blazing through flamehaired
nettles, so many,
such very brief stories.
For you I deciphered them:
a timeline entire, Craske
after Craske, gone topsy
and lichenous... taciturn
the black stone for the
foreigner... and Charlotte,
taken away, 5yr 3mo 4ds.

To forget; at last to be
half-forgotten. But one,
a sailor-boy shipped home
from Crimea, was restrained
still with pale flowers.
And you, 5yr and 3mo too,
that much and a dozen days,
were so quick to protest
on this level ground at
such a show of inequity.

Lifting a double fistful
and kicking up your heels,
you ran Craske to Craske,
pelting them with stars.
One bloom tigerish and
burning at the feet of the
black Dane. You invested
each mound. To Charlotte
you came last and grave,
and hemmed her long green
surplice with rosy petals.

We did not leave the way
we came, but side by side
through parkland thronged
and breathless, along a path
quite shiny with usage. At
times you dawdled, at times

danced. Dew on the grass.
Butter light. You stooped
and pressed a field-flower
between our palms. Down to
the water: you led me out.

LEAF-GIRL

Round and round the trampled
ground between the flaming
maple and the black walnut,
and out across the nickel rink
to the winter warming-hut,
round, round with bounds and
yells, skips and little rushes
you chased October leaves.

Curtsy, shout, leap and spin,
your pale face thin and hair
haywire, the best red-gold:
so you became the leaves
you caught. And watching you
I think I thought there's
some movement, some pursuit
best expressing each of us.

A PRAYER FOR JADE

You crouching
             and eyebright
(who have an eye always
for the tiny and particular)

and over the blades
of your fine shoulders
jade combers
             stropped
and spitting
and with heaven-bellows
                collapsing
into themselves

faint smile
                ginger tread
and you not quite
lifting the lid
of your long fingers
        on your secret
handful of transformations

maelstrom and mill
– spill over spill
               spraying
you with amulets

       precious shower

and you unmoved
            and still
half-bowed
intent on your fierce orisons

PORTRAIT OF A DAUGHTER

I'll draw you, my daughter,
in the shade beneath the tree,
so quiet you hear the world's voice,
so still you sense its moment.

No girl-in-the-green in oak leaves
with a passion of grass for hair,
no Rosie-round-the-haystack,
no yearning, egocentric Ophelia.

I see your head and shoulders
and whole body, nerve by nerve,
a host of troubled children,
some bloated, some skeletal.

This girl gnawing at a wrinkled breast;
this boy bawling at the empty sky;
this lump on the slow road;
this cheated meal for flies;

this bundle jolting on a cart;
this bald head; this threshing heart;
this bone-cage; this wafer;
this baby; these planet eyes.

You sit so still, you listen
so intently for each dumb child.
How can I draw you not sturdy,
not becoming as you are

but made of nothing more
than empathetic, wailing air?
Crouching hunger and dismay,
resignation seem to become you

as, taking them into you
– these poor ones, lost little ones
with only their lives to lose –
you grow into your own care

beneath the tree in the gloom.
I see you in your slow dream
learning, preparing, already near
the maze of responsibility.

Flowers you plant in others' wounds
seed themselves in you
and, looking up at me, you shine:
'I promise you. I promise.'

WALKING ON WATER

The first ragged frill
round the fringe of the lake
tinny and splintering before
you put half your weight on it.

The waterway itself
was still mulberry and slate,
it hadn't even started
to straiten round the dogged barges.

Ice-houses, lantern-bright,
and white hoods nosing out to them,
snowmobiles cutting
huge figures of eight:
all weeks and weeks ahead.

Yet this was the first
of the season's mysteries:
'Winter must come,
the pale sun will stand still.
Nothing we do or say,
no prayers our old mothers pray,
can quicken or avert it.'

Meeting, dry-mouthed,
at the water's edge,
breathless we talked too much,
we were so careful not to touch,
and stared aghast at each other.

In the blue hour
a flutter of snow
– no more than a dozen flakes or so –
the first November birds.

Then winter came where we stood:
teeth, traps, and fierce forecasts,
death-mists, sudden shinings.
But still we looked, still
we stared: the worst
of winter burned away
and it became so clear.

I could see the two of us
way out from this beginning;
in your gaze I saw us both
in our summer season,
hands linked, love-locked,
walking on open water.

PEARLS AND DIAMONDS

So the Queen of the North has lost her
baubles: pearlspawn, diamond scintilla.

In the sizzling cold little bundles
reel and stagger: the angels of the artists.
First they huddle in a scrum, then they
raise their arms and squeal, and stiffen
to fall back into the flowering snow.

The swimming moon rises, and like watercarriers,
lovers float through faded rooms.
They place tulips of white light, tall,
very slender, on ledges of high windows.

On the city sidewalks families blow
bubbles, and the dancers swarm and lift
– no colour, every colour. Then each
jewel catches night, it congeals,
goes dark and silently explodes.
'Look! Look!' Mica; precious dust.

More memory than presence, a woman
drags back her rhubarb velvet curtains
and traces patterns with a shaking hand:
pink peardrops, dazzling slabs, misty
blue teeth. Is Jack Frost the thief?

(And in the city margin, a literary critic
rubs his watering eyes: the Elders
in Chelm thought that treasure had fallen
from the sky; and at another time,
in another country, another queen
with a diamond incised syllables on glass.)

Spawn and scintilla. One man turns his back
on the revelations of the midnight city.
He lies on his bed, a stone on his stomach,
and dreams about the Queen of the North.
Her loss is legendary. On the cold
white page of his mind with love
he inscribes: winter-blossom; tears;
once and future seeds; merry dancers.

WHITE NOISE

Night swallows fumes from the mouth of the stack, and dusty knots
of creeper that half-covers the brick are sealed with ice.
Lowering your voice, you talk about fireflies, all kinds of owls,
dim creatures on the slimy bed that never swim, they reach and slide.
The standard first and then seven tulips long-necked in the window:
you turn off all the lights to hear the sounds of falling snow.
All we hear at first are the animal sounds of ourselves
– our hearts' iambs, and blood whistling round our heads, our coarse
breathing.
And snow that past midnight we scarcely see falling
except on an uptide, dancing on our window ledge, continues to fall.

Outside and shapeless, we shuffle like ancients block to block…
This wind's from the east: cottonwoods blossom, chastened cars
take the veil, and each cable fitting wears a busby and plume.
Motors and treads, party laughter on the doorstep, the tolling bell:
they're dampered like dreams, they sound like memories of
themselves.
A muffler's laid over the whole huge engine of the city.

Immoderacy! I slip and drift, and believe we have no destination
and will never reach one, and that's only the beginning.
There is something white stars say to you
and you throw off all the night to hear the sound of falling snow.
As we walk the watches, still the underhum withdraws,
exhausts and conditioners, fans and vents withdraw
until in the hour before dawn there is this:
this almost nothingness;
you, floating;
the sound of silence deepening, which is white noise.

LIGHT WEATHER

To such a morning
muddied language (even the clod
of consonants) is inappropriate

– so are self-important passages,
unblinking owl-faces
and the god of the Old Testament.

Beside the island runway
the little spring aeroplanes
sniff the air.

Not a cloud in the sky,
and spry launches breeze
across the harbour

where circles and strings
of white buoys bounce.
This lick-and-spit's electric:

the lake water keeps opening
her pale hands
and flashing her secrets.

To such a morning
all our shortcomings
seem virtually redeemable;

disappointments are hung out to dry
and our shared history
is just a flawed first version.

High above the lighthouse
the ringed-bills are making
an open weave of wind.

The lake's blue shoulders
slope and bend;
I recognise this world is a sphere

and to the patient and persistent,
mindful of a dream,
chance must come circling round again

on such a morning
as, flying out of winter,
you hurry to me here

and, on the island,
the willows and scarred cottonwoods
murmur in their buds.

COUNTING HER STEPS

She would still enjoy a head-to-head
with Heidegger, but not the waiting for it.
Her ardour for the sensual kept well in check
(say, chaste Lucie Rie) is no less pronounced
than it ever was, and her rejection
of the less than excellent uncompromising.
A gift for metaphor – and a sense
of humour. I can praise this woman!

But anxieties make her hoarse: her health;
the whole estate of her children. Her hair
is silver and ash, and downy as a cygnet.

Today she told me that on her constitutional
– and all day golden rods and storm clouds,
charcoal and indigo, and swirling leaves –
she counted her soft steps. One by one.
'Two thousand three hundred and ten,' she said.

True, she went on to ruminate on aspects
of the mile, beginning with the stride
of the centurion. But how easily she tires.
She sips and sups no more than a sparrow.
Is this how she begins to simplify:
counting and recounting the sum of her steps?

CLAY, SYLLABLES, AIR

*In celebration of the life
of Dick Crossley-Holland*

not is
past tense

past time
and warm

tears are ours
this spring

and lemon
morning

Let us make a man from syllables.
I say his eyes will be sapphire blue.
You were going to say the same thing too.
I say like David – Michelangelo's –
he'll have long arms, long legs, big toes.
You praise his proportion: head, hands, feet
and say he'll make a fine athlete.
We can agree and disagree;
prediction is like this, and memory.
Let us make a man from syllables.

Let us make a mind, let us make a heart.
You say he'll do right and never great wrong.
I say he'll always sing the right song
or stay silent: what I call natural grace.
You say he will be brave, and face
all weathers with equanimity.
I say true teacher; kind and witty.
You say a man who will love his wife,
his three children – who will love life!
Let us make a mind, let us make a heart.

And we will invest this man with air.
A subtle compound. I say he'll need
a mouthful – a sailor's daily creed
brought from mid-ocean. And you say smoke:
ring upon ring of Gitane, a blue cloak.

I say that mix of salt, iodine and mud
– let Nelson's air, Burnham air, sing in his blood.
Then may this creature of clay inherit
rushing breath: the holy spirit.
And we will invest this man with air.

      morning
      and lemon

      this spring
      tears are ours

      and warm
      past time

      past tense
      not is

FROM THE HALL OF THE AUTUMN PRINCE

How can I stand the cicadas?
Raucous as the dead.

I see a silver needle of air
above my head.
It will spiral through my fontanelle.
I shall not go mad.

When... when I...
gristle in my throat.

When I become king
I shall legislate against the past
and sanctify the new.
The court will be convex
and I shall be surrounded
by inventors and babies.
As soon as a woman has suckled her firstborn
her nipples are to be shorn
– likewise the testicles of the father.

No one in the kingdom will be
as old as I am.

Bodies are to be burned,
ashes scattered.
Headstones will be forbidden.

How can I stand these cicadas?
I will have them netted and boiled,
all the dusty pines they squat in
are to be hacked down.

Do away with the sidling lizard
and its wicked ancient look.

I shall not go mad.

How many?
How many days?
There is shame in waiting,

the hot wind hisses
the same words again and again.

I will discriminate
against all likenesses
and comparison and memory.

Nothing is to remain of him.
Let the shrieking birds
carry him and his shade
out of the kingdom, high over the waters.

He is dead already.
This is the kingdom of the dead hand.
Hollowed steps, withered olives,
and all the little rancid shrines.
Husks of ritual.

I will do away with his foul dispensations.
He chokes on his own obsequies.

Cicadas. Cicadas.
I will keep my years young
with what's new and disposable.
I shall not go mad.

Scrape the ground clean of shards!
Roll out the shocking pink
when I... I

THE FOX AND THE POET

Please tell me please. How chancy is it
for a young fox to meet a hungry poet?

A poet! It's time you were properly versed.
Of all our enemies the poet is the worst.

Worst! I thought poets were just amorous,
devious and gaseous, penurious – but glamorous.

They're shape-changers. They dream and devour.
They translate you and take away your power.

Don't tell me please. If he catches me,
what will happen if some poet bandersnatches me?

You'll be locked behind words. Cribb'd; confin'd.
Howling you'll run to the limits of the mind.

TRANSLATION WORKSHOP: GRIT AND BLOOD

Hige sceal þe heardra, heorte þe cenre,
mod sceal þe mare, þe ure maegen lytlað!
Word-stand, locking shield-wall
not to be broken down, nor even
translated in its own bright coin.
Courage, intention, resolve – won't do.
Out with Latinates! I want earth-words,
tough roots: grit and blood, grunt, gleam.

Harder heads and hearts more keen,
spirits on fire as our strength flags!
Here lies our leader, axed and limp,
the top dog in the dust. He who turns
from this war-play now will mourn
for ever. I am old. I'll stay put.
I'll lay my pillow on the ground
beside my dear man, my loved lord.

ALFRED IN THE ALPS

From Wantage. From Winchester. Under my tread the path unwinds.

Emerald and garnet and amber and jet. Upward, season-step. Pearl and swansdown. The stumbling king and his working men, his fighting men and praying men.

The immodest sun has shone for a week. He disarms the impossible peaks. He shouts at God himself.

The string-thin paths are crazed, the watercourses rusty and silent. Mountain-men we meet have skins creased and cracked as the skins they wear. My eye-balls ache, they're growing too large for their sockets.

But now at last the weather changes. I think we'll walk through clouds all day. Old habits. Dear unknowings.

I'll sleep, as I used to sleep, in the third hour after noon. And they'll tell me a butterfly danced out of my mouth. I will believe them.

I am of England. And I have cousins in Aabenraa and Brugge. I have friends in the Baltic and Arctic, where world's alphabet begins.

Chill days, dank evenings! The mercy of mood and change. My heart leaps with the eager orange-blue flames. Horses stamping. Woodsmoke tart and sweet.

Look at the shape-changers: dragon, sweet dancer, you cannot quite grasp them, ivory and oyster and lime and ash. Now they lift, and half-peaks soar and tumble.

I can hear my men tripping and cursing, finding their feet again. But they're climbing, still climbing: crossing the Alps.

South, the sun scarcely blinks, living is too easy. Vineyards. Misty purple grapes. And pampered men, impenitents, halfblind to the old imperatives.

Where's the true tip of the spear when oranges and lemons grow on the loggia?

My men should not go harvestless, my weeping women hungry; my little ploughchildren should not stiffen with cold. But some hardship's the best mulch. Give me high latitudes to grow spirit-fruit.

Think of the glory of the old oak. Listen to his painful story.

I'll wear this wrap of sopping mist. I'll watch this one dissolving crystal star. In this high wilderness, I do not ask for sight but to learn how to see.

Greece is ashes and Rome dust. There is no yesterday and tomorrow is too late. Lord, what is it you require of me this day?

THE VIKING FIELD

Not only thistles.

Gossamer: a shining network
woven before dawn.

Obstinate couch-grass
tall and blond
manning the ditches

and roses
tougher than they look,
craning their necks in hedgerows,
pale, shallow faces
following the sun's arc.

Scent of stone
and basting clumps of cow-dung.
Good warm glue.

A crinkle of silver foil
in the far corner.
Blind eye
flashing like a field of broken ice.

Day's breath bated.
Grass growing. The sound of it.
Sound of wool
growing on the lamb's back.

Systems of ants
stream out from their quarters
to inspect the field.

And even now
no dragons are forecast
for tonight,
but the candid sky
begins to congeal and sag.

Clover.
Wild garlic.
Ragged, unscrupulous crows.

Lance-leaves and heart-leaves,
tawny hairs, stinging.

Then all these spirit-wings:
this flickering assembly,
each silent woman flying
on her own
double-headed axe.

THE OLD MONK: VALLE CRUCIS

Under Fron Fawr
the wings of our old sycamore
whirligig again –
they're brittle and brown.

Huge carp skulk in the underworld.
The whole stew's alive
with glides and grins.

Saturday night
Brother Garmon and I
saw the floating bones
of Sister Linnet,
we heard her white skull singing.

Fron Fawr.
Almost half her green skin gone.
Purple for a season.

When I sit at this grille
the mass of the beetling hill
wholly occupies it.

Look at the sheep
perched on the escarpment:
dun and bright,
in and out of sunlight.
Look at the crown
and the rumbustious clouds

toppling over it.
I've grown so old and
it's halfway to God.

IN LATTER DAYS

After two or three
had gathered in His name,

the purring began.
Showers of bright semi-quavers
and the mountains skipped,
floods clapped their hands.

In the great emptiness,
on your knee-bones,
you dreamed about decay
and holy mildew
all over chiming England.

Again we sang;
then an officer trundled up
to the savage lectern
with his babyfood bible.

O ye gods...

Divine authority,
our fathers' cadences,
and their fathers' fathers,
shuffled off.

Committee-speak!
The work of the worthy
with flat feet,
fearful of fire and unknowing.

In the terrible gloom
you lowered your head,
accomplice
while the Word
was betrayed by the word.

THE ALDEBURGH BAND

Somehow a mouth-organist
has got into the flue
of the gas stove in the Baptist Chapel.

Every minute or two
she draws a plaintive chord
that dies as the north-easterly
roars in the stack
and the blue flames leap.

But it's in the gazebo
painted star-white,
all the benches wet with mist and fret,
that I recognise what's happened:

when the timpanist plays hide-and-seek
and beats his tiresome tom-tom
in whichever cubicle I'm not,

I soon see or, rather, hear,
the whole ragged band
is billeted piecemeal
around Aldeburgh.

So, for instance, the fat man
with the alpenhorn
has found his way into the massive
stone head of the sea-god –
Aegir, president of the flint-grey waves
– and he keeps bellowing in my ear
every time I pass him.

There's a pretty lutanist
behind that lattice window
on Crabbe Path;
whenever she leans out,
she runs her light fingers
along the modillion.

And the contralto with the treacly voice:
there's no escaping her!
She's always under sail, beating
up and down the windy High Street,
decked in globs of amber.

But where's the maestro
– some say magician?
Is he locked in the foundation
or under the long-eared eaves, still
tuning in?
The Aldeburgh Band:
did he have a hand in this?
Those who tell don't know.
Those who know don't tell.

Darkness comes in to land and I walk
along the beach
past the very last silent fisherman
with his lantern
and ghostly-green umbrella.
Crunchcrunch under my feet. Crunchcrunch.

Down to the water's edge
and still the music's everywhere:
all the strings night-bathing
and phosphorescent,
playing glissando;

the stray with the cor anglais,
lonely as a whimbrel
over dark water;

and far away,
far under the glagolitic ocean,
the now-legendary player
of the tubular bells.

FOOTSORE, IN SEARCH OF A CHINESE CELLIST

Mouth leathers, heels blister
in fluttering Burwood
on the first day of spring:

she's not at St Mary's;
not at Uniting. Not even
the Church of Christ the King.

High in the dry palms
the cynical laugh
and bright parakeets sing:

Hey, man! You, mister!
What have you come for?
Where are you going?

I've come from the true north,
come to hear grace notes
and run round in a ring.

It's now or never,
and so it is never.
Tomorrow's the Boeing

over the outback,
muzak and movie, the body's
high shine and breathtaking fling.

Tongue-tied I had listened
while young woman old cello
fused and took wing –

thighs, elbow and bow,
chestnut and tight gut:
a new kind of being.

(Her teeth were jagged,
and her mouth a poor purse,
her ankles were Ming.)

Mouth leathers, heels blister,
and I've searched every church
for the girl from Beijing.

Not a wrist or a bridge,
not one note, not a haunt;
no, not even a quivering string.

SELF-PORTRAIT

Thin white line and knot
on the forehead, quick to flare
– a medal conferred by a croquet mallet
on the upswing fifty years ago.

Nose tipped with a spare piece of putty.
Thistlefield of a chin,
highly competitive.

The folds of the eyelids
confidential, not quite epicanthic.
Ears almost Carolingian!

Eyes expressive; always inhabited.

Mouth shapely, concealing a canine
capped and painted in subtle tinges
– milkblue, oatmeal, cucumber flesh –
by a Bavarian dentist.

(Look! A face is a face.
What did you expect?
This quality, that defect
– the whole bag of tricks?)

Expression in repose: somewhat worried.
Professor from the cradle
with a silver head
tilting forward, a little to the right;
an earnest of concentration.

THE SECOND ATTENDANT

No reason to exaggerate.
It was never the Queen of the Night
I saw in the hellhole
of Liverpool Street
but her Second Attendant.

The train she disembarked from
was sixty-five minutes late
(Intercity: drawn by Halley's Comet)
because she brought on a heart attack in Carriage B
and then pulled the red chain.
Naturally.

Half-term holiday
and the previous train cancelled.
Passengers profuse and rank.
Well! as one man said,
at least the poor bugger
was spared the return journey.

As soon as the gang
in yellow hardhats spotted her,
they greeted her with wolf-whistles
and salvoes from pneumatic drills.
She conducted them
and laughed uproariously.

She was wearing a dress so black
it was green.

When she stooped
and fluttered the pretty red ribbon
two little children
couldn't resist her!
They dared the short cut over
the wet cement,
one wheeling the other.
She grinned and shook her head.

As for the stampede
and the ten thousand pools,
some gun-metal, some liverish:
child's play for this woman,
dressed as she was to kill.
The passengers could
scarcely take their eyes off her.
She made quite a splash!

And all this, she knew,
was just an overture.
Sky trembled.
Between high panes
the Dark Queen began to spit.

Arching her eyebrows, and far
from satisfied,
the Second Attendant
advanced on untold London.

HEAVY WEATHER IN HINTERTUX

Hunched over draughts on a chequer-board carpet,
oatmeal-rubbing, and glooming on the balcony,
ill-attuned to the idiocies of Radio Tirol
in the silly season: this is the sum of it.
Virgins in dirndls have limited charms.
It's down to the grotto and a long arm at kegel.
A bottle of obstler is the only quick way out.

Klammer and the ski-kings never showed up
and the Slavic trainers have squelched down
from the glacier. Cuckoo-mournful, cowbells toll.
Threading through ashen reaches and needles
– summer grazing, misty escarpments that
thrilled generations of poets and painters –
wanderweg and pfadspur clear their throats.

Deserters, departures! Out of this shining
cloud the butcher and his mutton wife go west
in their Mercedes, lean skis clipped to racks,
and the parkplatz looks quite cavernous.
Survivors become porous: sad containers
amongst the sopping hay-hedges, turning blue
with self-referrals, part of the place's lung.

TWO NOCTURNES FROM THE WILDMAN

Song of the Nine Waves

Wave-roam, wonder-home –

Wind-push, moon-pull, breath upon breath –
Mother! Mother! Ploughed deep silver –
Cradle, cry-life-lane, gambolling grave –
Star-glass, summer-breast, furlong-leap, life-beast –

Wave-roam, wonder home –

Wild kiss to cancer, caress to kill –
Paws, spines, glitter-thistles, quartz blooms –
Sea-shift, shape-change, candid, spellbind –
Syllable, somersault, salt-glazed tongue –

The Tide, Rising

Drawn-dreep, shell-shine, heart's tide rising –
Rumouring, memory, sheenskin ripple –
Fingers, obsidian, asking all knowing –
Spark and spearflash, sea-serpent, hiss –
Gossip and knock, knock, wave-whack, plunge –
Rib to furrow, salt-surge, ocean-rut –
Overlap, overrun, overcome, undermine –

NOTES ON A FIELD-MAP

in memoriam Cash Martineau

Corrugated and clouded,
many acres foxed,
face up in every season.

rookwing to mushroom

The Little Ouse still oozes
through Gallant's Meadow.
Fenced and throttled.

mushroom to muck

Badwell Hill Meadow.
Here I whistled Tempest
down the generous ride.

muck to chestnut

Bales of wild silk.
And the plump does
up-ending into their warrens.

chestnut to straw

Under light's blinding eye
boundaries, features,
characters all faded.

straw to chert

Here is Bull's Croft,
First Beeches. Second...
Felled. Gone to ground.

chert to pigeonwing

  ome   ado
This was Home Meadow.
Silver dust.

ANASAZI WOMEN

And with whichever story you come,
from whichever quarter or time,
the signs here mean the same.

Rock, clay, how they speak to us.

And as if from pink-brown pouts of cliff
snake-tongues of water
have slipped down, dripped down

and passing through themselves,
running through string-thin runnels,
the narrowest canyons of their own making,
grooved the high mesa, every limb:

shin-deep,
knee-deep,
thigh-deep,
hip-deep.
The passage of feet feet feet
rubbed away this white rock.

Women of clay,
sooty-lunged,
fingertips and palms
spiked by cactus,
how could they make these tracks?
Were they so blade-ankled
and slender-hipped?

Pots on their heads
heavy with hominy, pumpkin flesh,
were they so high-stepping,
knees to wasp-waists, each foot
placed directly in front of the other?

On this neck
high above the talus and twisted cliff-rose,
one petal of flint,
milk-white and deadly.
And look!

A sandal of crushed yucca leaves,
fringed at the toes.
Soft footfalls, fit for spirit-roads.

Women of clay, bearers of water.
Abalone in the sunlight.
Sweet song
of the wingbone of the golden eagle
crossing time.

And up top, as if the bandit wind
wields some giant rake with silver tines,
all the scruff and hardscrabble
is striated.
and scrub oaks rasp.
And where wrens flute
and loop,
the ground is stiff with sherds
– not sloping shoulders, slender hips,
not the little feet of dishes or fingerdips,

but all that remains
of pots proud-breasted and wide-hipped,
pot-bellied pots like melons and gourds,
ample, kind and porous.
Cream slip,
black slip,
orange on sepia,
mouth wide, womb-wide,
round as this poor planet
we make, and break.
How gently she rocks the globe
in her net of hair.

And the women:
bones of the women,
carters of corn and buffalo-fat,
hordes of gnats
gyrating around them:
all misshapen, ricked by arthritis;
their shining teeth
are ground down to their gums.

Neither tall nor slender,
not lanky as foal or fawn,
but thickset, short, stalwart:
poor imitations
of their own healthy pots.

Women of clay, Anasazi women.
High-stepping
through passage and cut,
crack and cleft
up and down from the windy mesa,
they left a dancer within warm rock.
Her feet tap, her fingers click,
time has not turned down her smile.

And there is a piper
lifting life's music,
replaying it to heaven.
Rock-woman, earth-woman,
coiled, almost foetal,
almost ready to spring out and stand,
singing-and-saying
and and and

Poems from East Anglia (1997)

IDLING

The way waves fold into themselves, sigh, then
play themselves out high on the foreshore,

a man draws and redraws the crescent contours
of the salt-woman he loves to draw to love.

PUPIL

Way to go the same way I went yesterday.
This way I see more: each blackberry,
each Norfolk reed – more plump, less plaintive.

Way to stare into the world's eye and see
its quick reflections; the pupil of now.

TO THE EDGE

To the scatter of a hamlet where nothing happens,
slowly. Sixty generations banked in the mud of
dogged minds.

To the scruffy hem of a rhomboid: acres torched and
charred. And far off as childhood the boy with
Punch and plough now a man astride his scarlet tractor.
Trawler of a torque of yelping gulls.

To the bounding lane. Skimmed and lumpen. Spinning
balls of gnats; matted honeysuckle. Acid in the
elderflower, old-fashioned Albertines athwart an
unhinged gate: those were the days less happy than
we think they were.

To the empty paddock and salt-crusted wall, the glossy
guarded holm-oaks.

To Mother Creek, flowing and flowering: her Byzantine
dark fingers laying open the marsh. The pools and
pulks are orange and sepia and slate-blue. Silt. Salt.
Yap of rigging. All the old arguments.

To a spur that's ragged. Beyond the leaching chemicals
and uprooted hedges, to the crossing-place where soil
and saltmarsh meet.

To a floor of uneven flagstone, filmed with beeswax.
Unfounded. Well-trodden. Flanked by clods of flint,
rough lime mortar.

Look at sun's fierce lances, the dance of light on
stone: word and spirit have reached an agreement.

The smell of mud and rose. You know you can still
tune this world: the way the mind infiltrates, ideas
assemble as if of themselves; the heart's pluck;
ancient, inner voices.

To an innocent page, damp and salty, and this fitful pen.

To the edge that's always chill and uncomfortable.
Tall reeds sing in the ditch. Tide turns against
the wind, bucking and amber and hilarious.

Selected Poems (2001)

FOUR CAROLS

1 The Nine Gifts

I bring you my body, darling dear:
My ripening song, my jubilant ear.
That's what Mary sang. *Alleluia*!

And I bring surprise – this sweetest fragrance
Made with love and hope in patience.
That's what Elizabeth said. *Wonder*!

I come with a trill and a blue light
And followers stumbling through the night.
That's what the star sang. *Rrrrr*!

Well, my lamb, I've got you this fleece
So your old mother can get some peace.
That's what the shepherd said. *Yan! Tan*!

I bring you the broken tooth of a giant,
No compromise, the word that is silent.
That's what the stone seemed to say. ( )

I bring you guffaws and loops of mist
And a band of brown hair for your right wrist.
That's what the donkey said. *Eeyore*!

I bring you my crown and an uneasy dream
Of duty and honour, gossip and scheme.
That's what the king said. *Heigh-ho*!

Open your hand for this fitting glove:
The name of the song in my throat is love.
That's what the ring-dove sang. *Coo-oo!*

But what can I bring you. I bring me.
Whatever I am and all I will be.
That's what the child sang. *Little Jesus!*

2 Pilgrim Jesus

Iesus! Christus! Iesus! Natus!

In the manger of my body
Leaps the tiny child, and his breath
Is the word – the dance of God.

Corpus! Beatus! Peregrinus! Natus!

In the ocean of my head
The steadfast ship rides tide and storm
On its pilgrim crossing.

Oceanus! Peregrinus! Christus! Natus!

In the orchard of my heart
Springs the singing tree. Its root
Is faith and its sweet fruit charity.

Cor! Arbor! Amor! Christus!

Riding ship, springing tree,
And in the manger leaps the child
Who is the word – the dance of God.
Iesus! Peregrinus! Iesus! Natus!

3 The Heart-in-Waiting

Jesus walked through whispering wood:
'I am pale blossom, I am blood berry,
I am rough bark, I am sharp thorn,
This is the place where you will be born.'

Jesus went down to the skirl of the sea:
'I am long reach, I am fierce comber,
I am keen saltspray, I am spring tide.'
He pushed the cup of the sea aside

And heard the sky which breathed-and-blew:
'I am the firmament, I am shape-changer,
I cradle and carry and kiss and roar,
I am infinite roof and floor.'

All day he walked, he walked all night,
Then Jesus came to the heart at dawn.
'Here and now,' said the heart-in-waiting,
'This is the place where you must be born.'

   4 *Jesus, Springing*

I am the heart that houses the cone
I am the cone enclosing the cedar
I am the cedar sawn for the cradle

forest of the body
body of the tree

I am the cradle rocking the baby
I am the baby containing the man
I am the man nailed on the cross

tree of the body
body of the forest

I am the cross sawn from the cedar
I am the cedar enclosed in the cone
I am the cone housed in the heart

here in my heart
Jesus, springing

LIKE A SMALL SIGH

Along the thin line
                    of light under your bathroom door
I see your cat stretch and bow down. She makes
strange little noises deep inside her throat
until you admit her to your steamy sanctum.
That is the first I know of today
except for snow ploughs grinding and cackling
like a skyful of rooks
opening the frontiers
between night and morning. I am half a dream away.

With right hand, left leg, I claim your side
of the bed. The sheets are warm and silken.
Then it's the spit-and-flush of your shower,
wrapping me, pre-natal, until as usual the Nutrigena
slips from your slick fingers and hits the deck.
You say as soon as you step out the cat jumps in
and laps and licks the whole tub dry, every drop.
I can understand that.
                    When I open my eyes
again, you've reassembled in our little bedroom.
Naked sylph wearing nothing but a white turban,
little more than an outline in the feeble
light beginning to leak between the slats.
You are so narrow at the hips.
                    You bend, I can
scarcely see the groove between your apple-buttocks.

Disciple at a dark drawer, you fuddle over what
and mainly what not to wear: this white, that black.
No, white! Now over them your silken magnolia slip.
Such care; such hesitation.
                    What is more doubtful,
more lovely to watch than a lovely woman, dressing?

5.30 exactly and the telephone rings
                    – not a fax
from England, as happens often, but quick fire
from a friend: the roads are too icy; freezing fog;
or freezing rain. Yup! Your school opening's
delayed for two hours.

You whoop me up, and then
at once you penguin down the passage to the kitchen.
Not listening, I listen to your ancient
radio's crackling confirmation: Saint-Croix,
Catholic Springfield, Sauk Center, Stillwater…
Another call, another colleague and a second volley.
'I'm back to bed,' I hear you say.
            Incautiously,
you peel away your silk skin. Ribs of white light!

You enter the bed like a small sigh,
and still we've exchanged not a single syllable.
At first you turn away, hook your left ankle
over my left heel.
            One breath! You dream yourself
deep into curves, almost imperceptibly.

AND GOD SAID

My work! It is so beautiful
And they did not realise it.

So I made monkeys of them,
Tipped loads of morning duty over them,

Turned the knife in their sides until
Each petal of blood was unbearable.

*

I hurt because they hurt me:
They could not see me clearly.

So I put into their eyes the gauze
Of morning mist in the valleys

And a double measure of pain. Still
They cannot see me clearly.

*

Syncategorematic! How clever they think
They are. True, I will not strip them

Of my word, but they keep wrapping
Themselves in words of their own.

Thousands of beatitudes, millions
Of platitudes stand between us.

*

But sometimes the scales fall from
Their eyes. They stare at green hills,

Their swelling breasts, and indolent clouds
Stooping over them. Innocent again

Of all they perpetrate, they dream
And almost know what I intended.

*

They are not just one of my rehearsals
And each day they grieve me.

How they bleat and snort and bray
And lay one another's mates.

Nerve gas, bombs, land mines!
I was right to fix their term.

*

During their dark season trust went
Into hiding: they wrote thoughts on air

And tried out their own nightmares.
Some were needed for crocodile meat.

But I have given them generation.
A few I have ennobled to say no.

*

I have bandaged their wounds with illusions.
They think their hurt is mortal,

They believe their suffering improves them
And are convinced they can change nothing.

They say I have told them
They will live again after they die.

*

I see poets – a whole unreliable army
Of egotists, promiscuous and unstable.

I am the yeast, I am the priest,
I am the alchemist, I am the conscience...

Listen to them! Do they really
Think they will have the last word?

*

How they go on searching for me.
Like lovers on love's threshold

They stare until their eyes burn,
And suppose they almost see me.

As if I were hiding from them
– gargantuan, dressed in skirls of cloud.

*

Taut nipple, shocking pink stem,
Loops and ropes of indigo and flame

And scarlet blossom folding in
On itself: all this before leaf-rattle,

The mouldering and dung beetle.
The fools! I gave them eyes to see.

*

Let my children hear each speckled leaf
Sing a song no less singular

Than their own. Let them enter
Into understandings with water and earth

And each unblinking stone.
Are these not ways back to me?

*

They are so powerless, so afraid
Of knocking night. Look how they sow

Seeds of stammering light
Halfway up the flank of the dark mountain.

– Ah! Had I not chosen I would
Still choose to assure and shelter them.

*

Where they are, I am.
I will always prevent them.

And whatever looks into their eyes
Will divine their song without ending.

But I will release them. How can I
Deny them the mercy of time?

*

Who watch the crying world wide-eyed,
Without averting their gaze. Who keep

Faith through the fatal night.
Who accept all they think they cannot change

But move when they move with the rhythm
Of purpose. My own children!

*

What opposes grace? Disgrace.
And brutality? Tenderness.

How can hate mother love?
What is the distance from no to yes?

They live in these interstices.
I live in all their choices.

*

Sometimes I think I did not dream it
Entire but only in night's shallows,

And say I have always failed them.
Sometimes I gaze at the curvature

– such shining, such darkness –
And believe that this is still my dream.

*

I watch how they deceive themselves
And deceive one another.

Since they have cast me in their image
They suppose they can deceive me.

And because I have set them free
They cry I have deceived them.

*

They test me with their anguish,
The fearsome hound of their hunger,

Foul diseases that disfigure them,
Worst, their sullen armour of indifference.

I cannot turn them away. Like them,
I change nothing. I suffer their suffering.

*

There is another darker dream
I cannot contain. Is it because

I have chosen not to come close
To them, or because they are not constant,

Or because of their wild beauty,
I trouble myself I am their dream?

LIMOGES

All I knew of Limoges was my mother's china:
teacups transparent as raised communion wafers,
with knuckled twig-handles, their gilt half-worn.
Shining bone miracles tough as old boots.

When the night train pulled in, quacking,
it was damp and chill. One frail old woman,
coiffed and frilled, peered out from her kiosk.
Hooded eyes. Top lip stitched. Time to kill.

ANASAZI

Where altitude snags
                    our breath
pink rocks writhe.
They scald our fingertips,
and she-pines underswish.

This is where she gasped...
and he fired spirit-arrows....

We cannot quite run these people to earth,
least of all by turning over each stone.
Even written words weigh much
                                  too much
when ruins are so little more than
rearrangement
of the place's bones.

Here is the human abattoir...

Up against their overhang
vultures catch thermals.
How hungry they are
for life, cresting
                    and swooping,
hurrahing through groves of gamble-oaks,
cinders in the valley.

Orchard of little peaches...

So where is the song
of that hidden bird
                    leading us?
Canyon wren?
We are not even sure of its name
but have come to recognise the tune.

Curious and careful,
                    we are here,
and they know we are.

from **SWARM AND HONEYCOMB**

in memoriam Margaret Douglas-Home 1906-1996

2 Saints of the Foreshore

Who hum among bee orchids, wink and
wilt again with each wilting sea campion.

Who heard the German Ocean rasp, and suffered
draughts, damp cold and like punishments.

They grew into ground, stay-at-home pilgrims
drawing near with faith in the company of seals

and avocets; partners in stubborn understandings
with thrift and anguished hawthorn-trees.

Rinsing ascetics at the head of foundations
and kindly teachers of knock-kneed novices;

contemplatives islanded in their own cells,
distillers of sweetness, harvesters of God.

Celtic mothers and Saxon fathers: their piety
most enviable because uncomplicated,

though hard-won. But who said anything
should be easy? Not the crusted stanchions

on the foreshore, nailing together earth, sea, sky.

3 Jesus of Norton

Infant of the bubbling spring
well in my heart.

Child of the sighing marsh
breathe in my head.

Son of the keen light
quicken my eyes.

Rebel of the restless creeks
tumble in my ears.

Disciple of the rising tide
dance in my heart.

Teacher of the gruff salt-wind
educate my tongue.

4 Half-Saints

Near as a heartbeat yet foggy and far
one bell swings in the high tower.
One heart beats and a modest crowd of folk,
some of them strong and all of them weak,
make a bee-line for church.
                              Collectors
of small change for good causes; doctors
of the heart; dependable helpers
who befriend the lonely; stitchers and quilters;
two Samaritans, not quite anonymous; makers
of church marmalades; aid-workers on leave,
leathery and haunted;
                              few of them known
outside their own communities, none heroes
or victims, but singular women, singular men
who expect the arduous and mundane
and avoid plaudits.
                              Lives of the spirit!
Bees circle them as they sleep.

5 Crossing-Place

This is the house of the unspectacular
and invisible;
                      the threshold of some dream
or of something we once knew.

   Kingdoms of the earth, sing to God.

This salt-bleached tower!
Who conceived it and who ordained it?

Who hired the master-builder and was he paid
on time? Who blessed the quoins?
Who moved the stone?

    Kingdoms of the earth, sing to God.

Pulpits, rood screen, Virgin in outline,
acanthus leaves:
                one gift for love
of God, another in memoriam;
this one a matter of appearances;
that, down payment on a passport to heaven.

    Kingdoms of the earth, sing to God.

To step inside time
by answering the pulsing bell
our grandparents heard
                and seeing stars
of sunlight at play on an ancient wall
is one way back, and forward;
to sense worn hands and lives
in fabric visionary or homespun
is to cross the threshold
                scalloped by love.

    Kingdoms of the earth, sing to God.

SALT-COMPOUNDS

salt-scythe
sweeps onshore, corrosive and hissing; pins back
ears; rifles each stay, shroud and halyard.

creek-wood
the old ones, clinker-built and always thirsty;
noses blunt and bottoms glaucous; still quivering.

sea-garment
roseate spinnaker, light-breasted; no less
stiff canvas, often split and mended, grey with salt.

herring-haunt
see-through escarpments toppling and barking
as they dive through themselves into ghosts of flint

mauve-mist
delicate as breath suspended over marsh grass;
summer carpet, wiry and tide-beaten, knotted in mud.

wave-arms
without joints, creaking and groaning; like wings
their strange spade hands salute and dip and rise.

mud-runes
ribbon-casts, blow-holes, keel-scrapes, anchor-spikes,
darts of the stitchers and strutters and mincers.

THE GRAIN OF THINGS

Beware of what's uniform, lapidary, slick.

As if a twisting country lane
where shadows bow and curtsy
were to be avoided
because of its green spine and blisters;
or it were desirable
that literary translations should not sound
foreign and close to the originals.

Waxen-skinned fruit is apt
to taste less sweet than the pocked potato
and ruckled pomegranate.

Let me have about me
not members of the awkward squad
or fools so cussed they cannot compromise,
but friends who think, and say
what they think, not given to repeat
themselves with variations;
men and women with robust wordbanks
who deal in things no less than intuitions
and cast their cloaks before the beautiful.

Salt-milled stone has its place.
Oil has its place.
Likewise the assembly line.

And no, I have no wish to be abraded
when I am low in spirits
or to listen to the litanies of the bigoted,
nor even to be pricked by the moustache
of an amorous woman!

But give me the gruff,
the honest stumble and crux –
the obstinate knot in the grain of things.

THE ART OF PICKING BLACKBERRIES

Containers seldom grow on trees.

*

Follow a hedgerow centuries
old. Hawthorn-and-lime, ash-and-sycamore
link arms, and through its bright windows
you glimpse once upon a time
– no more than a breath away.

*

Some berries are hairy; some have scabs;
some are perfectly formed but exceedingly small.
The juices of many taste diluted.
Choose refined but vigorous stock.

*

Be so peaceable the pigeon
attentive in the thicket
does not fluster.

*

Never wear gloves, like some murderer.
Expect purple thumbs and forefingers.
Expect blood.

*

Gather them still almost firm when
very gently you squeeze them:
those that come
away from their stalks a little reproachfully.
Embodiments of sweet asperity.

*

Victorian families of ten or twelve.
Fourteen!
But the firstborn grows misty, already sagging soft,
while some of the bunch are still rosy-cheeked,
and the little one hazel-and-green.
How many is it right to pick from the cluster?

*

n.b. And how many papulae,
this rounded, that faceted,
glisten on the body
of each berry?

*

Bindweed and nettles! Bryony and nettles!
Risk the sting and overreach
for that best one
you almost catch exposed and off balance.

*

Ignore the reticent sloes
(that gin still squats at the back of the cupboard)
and the punchbag hips
(chemists used to buy them: fourpence per pound).
Keep away from haws.

*

Now to extricate this hedge.
This one berry.
Fleeting breath on your cool brow;
yellow light; plumpness;
swollen fingertips, a little numb, not quite your own.

*

The art of picking blackberries is
to know when to stop.

Moored Man (2006)

MOORED MAN

Moored Man's Song

His feet are caked with creek mud,
his shins are indigo.

And yet Moored Man lifts his eyes
across the slakes, across the waste
and sees an island, riding.

His arms are tied with marram roots,
his thighs strapped with green weed.
He wears a fraying halter.

Moored Man lifts his grey eyes
and peers through iron-cold bars.

Colours of salt and honey.

He is half-old, tide-worn, wind-worn.
He roars and starts to sing.

Moored Man Almost Remembers

Sheen-eyed and unblinking, quick
to the creek's sudden lurches and quivers.

Undergrowling
at the far fierce crash and pound
deep day makes sullen.

Before all this.

Did he fall?

Was it a hundred wings with one will
raised him into air-tides?
When he swam and drifted. When he cried.

At dawn he rises from the groyne
under the barefaced sky.
His forearms shine and ripple.

Once more he braces his blunt thumbs
and sinks them into boulders.

One blue window in his mind.
One feather tarred to his left shoulder.

   Making the Island

Why?
Because it welled up – a single keen wave
out of the flatcalm of his mind.

He squelched and splashed north.
He waded out
a mile and more
up to his thighs, his hips.

Why?
To see felicity.

On the hazy bar he began.
With both feet he scratched and scraped
like a wild sea-cat covering its faeces,
until his ankles were bloody and raw.

Then he kicked. He kicked.

Why?
So the Polar reach
would end in his ears?

The gravel flew and dropped,
it swarmed and swirled like chaff
in the murky water.

Longshore drift did the rest.
Pebbles and grit swam
and settled in new stations.
They rose above themselves
out of the water.

Schschschhh-huh!
Soft echoes in the cavern of his mouth.

Time and wind.

A shining cap of sand!
Sea-kale, tugging at its roots.
Sea-holly, growing beautiful
as it grows old.

Sss-sk! Sss-sk!
He strikes sounds on his sandpaper tongue.
Sss-sk! Tt! Tt!

The sun draws its blade
over his welling land.
Why?
Because it was not there.

He stares at his island
and knows he is beautiful.

Young Woman

He begins with her toes.
One by one
by one he massages them
and paints them silver-blue.

He applies indigo poultices
to her porcelain ankles.

Then he shows her his claws.
Scratches her shins all over, very lightly,
until she stands shivering under midday sun.

And kneels to him.

The further she comes
the more he grows towards her
and reaches out behind her.

The backs of her knees:
he tickles them with a feathery wisp.
And then he wraps himself around her skinny thighs:
bleached pink, lavender.

He is waiting for her at the hanging valley
and the dark pool.

She stares at herself in him.

Instead of a Roar

First he sees everything, then
narrows his gaze
to nothing but his fierce intention.

Three lolloping, laughing boys,
each blowing mist balloons
and stuffing them with loud words.
The point of his silence lies in wait for them

Next, the retriever walking his chapped mistress
and grinning:
for one the slip,
slime and mud-slurp for the other.

High on the dyke's shoulder
black pods rattle
and late bugs trundle over lank grasses,
The parcelled woman with sore eyelids
stumbles, sobs.
Wasteland of my heart, she thinks.

He is like the barn owl:
pouring out of himself upwards
and very fast, quietly
spreading the dark sheet of his shadow.

One disciple stands his ground.
He watches Moored Man for months; for years;
He sees through him.

Foreigners

Where are they always going?
Why are they coloured yesterday and tomorrow?
Foreigners!
Why do they have so little to do with him?

They goggle at him through binoculars
and chuck empties at him.
They swear at him and shit on him
because they cannot see him.

Moored Man is still glad, though.
He likes how they look,
and their looking at each other.

He likes his dreams.

When dark clouds laced with silver
gang round the sun
and shadow-ribs race away across the marsh
into the mudflats,

he sobs inside himself again,
unblinded and knowing
how they must have to do with him.

Waste

When they hurry through, eyes cockleshelled
against the savage light,
declaring they love him and what would they do
without him,

and how all summer
he was benelsoned
like Lady Hamilton's breasts,

and how his groynes
need more attention

all their words are only for themselves
and each other.

His heart aches.
His ears start to sing.

He watches three curlews work sobbing water,
he inspects the massive spar
dressed in stars of salt
with rot in its gut.

His bones – are they melting?
One day he feels almost weightless,
the next he sinks back blue
into himself,

and he broods
until the tide turns in him once more
and he could rise and ramp
before the howling wind
and blot out everything.

Unknowing

Pear and pale pink and oatmeal
 – he can see for miles
the southern rim breaking
into colour,
flaunting spring flags.

He can hear the taunts of golden trumpets,
and the piercing cries of children,
and young lovers sighing in their bones.

So pitted and pocked.
So invaded. So exhausted.
What is he
today but an old grey map again
crossing itself?

Moored Man grinds his heels. His teeth.
He cannot help himself.

He stamps
and his mud splatters the sky's pane.

He thumb-stops his ears.
Crouching, he sees nothing
for hailshot, for hot tears.

Moored Man's Plan

He sleeps with a stone on his stomach.
When wakes
he sees the upshot waiting for him:

crabs will sidle from their shells,
lobster pots turn themselves inside out,
mussels will play their castanets;
buoys will harness themselves in weeds,
saltwater and freshwater
will stand up and embrace.

What a dance!
Snub nose bucking, clinkers slipping anchor.
The price of disrespect.

First he must cock his ears.
He must listen
deep into the sound
of the sound where all sounds meet.

Next he must make of his own throat
and diaphragm a winding marsh-horn.

Moored Man's yawn: it is whale-wide.

The third thing. The third
will be the third thing
will...

Whale-wide; cloud-wide.
Again he falls asleep.

His Voice

Growling as he sleeps,
his own sinking world's ground-bass.

His voice is like the memory
of gunnery practice out at sea.

Dark brother
of the swill and pound and chatter
way beyond the cockle bight,
ocean's mouth
ancient and still promising
to deceive.

Witness

While he peels off his tatters, sodden
with dew, and tosses them into sky,

his tern flaps and hovers,
its javelin scream
white as the edge of the first morning.

What does he see?
A looming impression
in the creek's murky obsidian
and the flashy mudflats?

Can he see himself at all
in the green shoots bristling on the marsh,
the leprous rashes of sea-pink?

They see him.
They bear witness to him.

Naked he stands,
upright
where restless levels meet:

tall as a sun-lance,
a bright column striking,

while on an air-stream
his tern balances.

   Ablutions

He begins to stretch through himself
– his daily becoming.

Sharp blue teeth; flounders and flatfeet;
sudden sloshing.
Then the crook-necked grey one
Stabbing and gulping.

He stares at his skin's asterisks –
salt-crusted scars,
spatters of flowers like service-medals –
and lets each tide rise through him.

Once again the ruckled beds and lays
go under, and the soft mound, silver and grey,
around the freshwater spring.

Each day he rises,

and over his head
the light grows fearsome.

   Trickster

As though he were the son
of apparent light and the mimic jay:

he quivers and glares,
he unrolls carpets of sticky mud,
then spits laughter as he laces
fine sand with pointed stones.

And as though he were screaming quicksilver:

he rises to the moon,
drags the lumpen tides
until the creek's swollen and impassable...

But tricksters turn to darkness.

He licks oozing blood,
rubs salt into wounds;
he cracks and snaps bones.
In the evening he drowns little children,
and then he howls with remorse.

Old and wild and angry,
child of mayhem, father of grief.

The Same Badge

When they inhale his minerals, their blood
fizzes. They soon grow giddy.

Standing on a mudslide spit
a young leftie casts his line, slips
and barbs his own right thumb.

Their slates are too good to lose.
Two boys playing ducks-and-drakes
skim them across the narrow creek
straight at one another's shins.

Now someone's daughter leaps
from Old Stoker's wreck,
drives her incisors through her lower lip.

Each summer victim wears his badge:
a ring of stinging iodine
around the leaking wound's mouth.

Before the Storm

What is on its way, massing
upstream, is like a tower about to topple
or a cloak of spelter bruised with purple.

And what is smooth-ironing
the afternoon's long sleeve
is his own stillness. Effortless his water

swans down midstream, softly
it backheels in the margins.

Each minute hangs and seeps. It trickles
through his myriad gorges of mud.

Birds cross very high, out of earshot,
and balls of gnats ferment
while still he dozes,
one glassy eye open,
until his sheer shine could blind you.

Storm's gonfanons hoisted and advancing,
Moored Man unhurried but at bay:
this perfect equilibrium
arrested
on the shield of the waiting day.

His Shadow, His Smile

When her own quicksands
snagged the woman on the foreshore
and, choking, she did all she could
to clutch her left breast,

Moored Man trembled until
his bone-joints cracked. His teeth ached.

Laser gulls tacked into the headwind,
shrouds and halyards keened;
low he stooped
and threw his long shadow over her.

Stopgo shrimps soon sized her up.
Come whiskers, come pincers!
Come terns and cormorants!

She was his golden cornstook,
she was his wave-cornflower
until the jade tide turned and made,
and beckoned her.

Gently Moored Man smiled
as the pale sun blinks and smiles
on the stranded and the breathless,
on the dark wave's welling
and winter wheat.

Searching for the Stone

On seventh days
his labour is to search for the stone.

He turns his back on the comfortable bells,
the silk-and-velvet cattle
stamping on each other's shadows.
First to comb the foreshore after high water.

Although it is there
it is never there
at first, and then as no more than a glint
in the corner of his bloodshot eye
He rakes the shingle beds beside the creek,
glares until each stone turns sepia.
Until pebbles crunch his brains.

And then
it is there.

Utter,
transparent and unblinking.

Between his rough fingers he holds it up.
He raises it,
free and shining,
quite clear of time.

But he knows what he has to do:
surrender the stone again to the sea tongues,
insistent and clamouring.
He draws back his arm,
hurls it, slings it
into the water's throat,
as far from him as it has always been.

Moored Man's Tides

He faces the offing and world's rim.
Home of the nightfall.

This bickering and sucking soft, this
lapping as tide grows heavy in itself,
then dies to be reborn:

how does it mean? How do tides mean?
This falling and rising,
moaning and thrust .

In his gut the puzzle bubbles and ferments
but still cannot surface.

If only he could spring it –

The welter; the rim;
the colours of separation;
always the ache of his tides
chiming
deep within.

Her in Him

He sees how she spreads herself.

The scallops of her palms,
the little blue hollows.
Her ribs – their pale crescents and sparkle –
and the clippings of pearly razor-shells.

Her salt-stiffened sprays of green hair.

Ankle-whip, shin-whip:
she wears skirts of wild silk
slit to the thighs.

Soft, stale O of the hagstone's mouth.

Each night the cold white flames
of the slakes and oozing meals.

Ghost-Light

Under the Milky Way
his hidden lips and little throats
open, they stay open
as he sips and gurgles.

Under the dark, burning spaces
he spreads himself and plots himself.
Prone and accepting.

He strops his blades
under the red star.
Like nerves his wiry hairs quiver.

Under the wrenching moon
he is slats of ghost-light,
he is ribs and rising.
All he is, all he was
in this dream of re-becoming.

Quite

No one knows.

Or, rather, everyone knows
but each tells a quite different tale.

Moored Man listens.
He sleeps with one eye open,
gauzy with death-mist.
He who hears the artillery
of popping bubbles, beetles tap-dancing
and the shooting scooters,
listens.

They were home on leave.
They were Home Guards.
Foreigners.
They were Germans.

Both men were wearing identical uniforms.
At Bank Hole, beside the groyne,

they stripped, or did not strip
but the sea stripped them, naked.

It's a day's dive to the bottom.
Diz with her webbed fingers and webbed feet
is the only one who ever touched it,

unless they touched it.
When the whirlpool dragged them down.

What of their stigmata?
Snagged, gashed on a spar's nails.
No! Drowned men split and tear.
No! They clawed each other.

Moored Man listens
until they are quite finished.

All everyone agrees
is both men were found floating,
they were lolling
side by side, moon-faces up.

    Saying

Saying:

I had forgotten as the old forget
this morning's deep charge:

plumbing each orifice,
gouging scum from my veins,
bursting my pockets.

All my pus and jetsam!
I will usher it
into the marsh
where now filters into then.

Saying:

I turn, I make, I flow, I come.
I also am young.

His Line

Headline. Heartline.

Line from once to will be.
Innocence to responsibility.

His skyline
murmuring
to west, to east.

His line about you
and now
if not always.

Marooned Man

Is this it?

Nothing barking; or breaking;
no chitter-chatter.
Nothing in the spire-shells of his ears.

Amongst the reeds of the freshwater creek
the chugging coots make not a sound;
neither does the sizzle of gnats.

He is cocooned and cannot see himself
in focus, only that he's dressed
in shining, sticky webs.

The gut's half-drained and listless.
His limbs are limp.
Nothing's bated.

Is this how it will be
– this erosion of the senses, and exhaustion,
one long ooze?

His skin is drenched,
his arms outstretched.

Yet he is smiling almost,
still alive, marooned, and unfree.

Attraction Water (2011)

GREEN SACRAMENT

Oh! Rockily, rockily
in a silver-green cleft squats the log-church
of the Seventh Day Adventists
presided over by pert Pastor Murtsch.

Luckily! Oh, luckily
his field-bishop's hip, a cool old bean
who gets where Murtsch is coming from
and why his trip's gone green.

Cockily, cockily! Oh,
Pastor Murtsch prepares his sons and daughters
to partake of the sacrament,
saying the words our Saviour has taught us:

'Take. Eat. This is my broccoli...'

ORISONS

Sagging so slightly now thirteen centuries
    of sky have encompassed her, curvature
quite smooth-skinned, pinned by rosy quartz:
    shore-hugger beached, granite keel uppermost,
flanked by hedgerows bright with God's tears.

Draw near but not too near. Where west wind
    snuffles, just peer through her port-hole
into the shining gloom. Look! Are the pilgrims
    not still at their tholes, moon-faced, falling, rising,
slowly bouncing almost, between here and heaven ?

Gallarus Oratory

NAVIGATORS

In this salt-fret, this unknowing,
the immigrants from Iceland
swirl and sheer
round this bright beacon,
our shining-eyed barn,
for the dear life of it.
Whose gang of brothers,
silver-grey, have strayed
far inland, and pink-footed sisters
come to shocking harm
among humming turbines.
Navigators of the watches.
Night-scythers, night-threshers,
honking and wink-winking,
instinct with dawn.

TRYING TO REMEMBER

Trying to remember what it was
I had to remember
which was not
all the ways I can see wind
– where it's coming from, breathing
now through gold-green tresses,
its changing shape –
and not to excavate
snails from the beech's black spout
before watering it
as I must do daily
during this drought, or even to count
the species feeding at the table,
between times inflicting grievous losses
on the crop of sweet peas,
already meagre,
parting them from ramping grasses,
that's when out of the corner of my eye
I saw you by my apple-tree,
more than a thousand miles away,
shaped by wind, green and thirsty,
honey-tongued, singing.

PORTRAIT OF A WRITER

Raymond Escholier 1882-1971

The stone table where they sit rounds on itself,
redoubtable and time-worn. It's dispassionate.

And the woman beside him, hair in a bun,
strappy shoes, she's inclined, not unadmiring.

About him their garden murmurs, self-seeding,
almost wild, always reaching and failing.

All these ease his generous brow, they almost just
-ify his jaunty bow-tie and indulgent half-smile,

but how well he knows – head, heart, hand –
that not with water nor bread, no with nothing

but his own words will he receive consolation.

WHEEL OF NORFOLK

This hubbub, all this hullabaloo: a romping northwesterly
rippling the pantiles, and our barn-hulk itself troubled
and booming, a silver torque of gulls screaming
around the scarlet tractor and the plough...

So where to begin? Not with an early field-map
– I can't locate one – otherwise I'd sing each airy acre.
With our seven Burnhams then, without forgetting
those half-forgotten: Saint Edmund, Saint Andrew, Ulph.

With people near as heartbeats: the Viking in his mound,
White Friars in their ruins; Dalmatian horsemen, freezing
and homesick, manning the green breasts of the shore fort
with a stroppy cohort – auxiliaries from Aquitaine.

Here's my spoke of light. Today it's chalky, blossoming,
weightless yet substantial, starting to seethe
as the wind runs out of breath. This is heaven's doorstep.
Gallow Hill looks ready to heave and take off.

And here's the spoke of colours, lit from within:
marsh-green and sea-lavender, marram, duck-egg, woad.
And now, these draughty, flinty churches, my stopping-places,
my taking-stock places, one my final destination.

Work (and the lack of it), summer visitors in shoals,
affordable housing; innocent by-lanes and decaying piles;
sugar-beet clamps, hectares of rape; Nelson and Coke
and half-a-dozen familiar names: each one's a spoke.

Here's the flight of the barn-owl who beats our bounds,
ghostlike and unhurrying, and all the small fry
(not only thirteen blackbirds) feasting in our beds,
these and threshing echelons on flight-paths to Scolt Head.

Chalk Hill. This is my hub, always still, always turning.
And here at home this morning I map my wheel of Norfolk.

GIANT JELLYFISH

Mainly throats contracting and dilating :
Mushroom concertinas rounding on themselves,
Wreathed in orange and tarnished silver frills.
Little Satans! Undersides splayed like long-haired
Shaving-brushes. Harbour harem swaying for
A vile dancing-master; a submarine eclipse,
Total and sideways drifting, seething indigo.

FELIX

True to your name.

Here you came bright-eyed
above the sombre valley
and sat dapper at your easel,
your inner ear attuned
to all that rises
above the vale of tears.

It is never wrong, seldom fruitless
to listen for the footfalls
of great women or great men.

Out of breath, out of tune
I rehearse again
what I scarcely believe
I could have forgotten,
the most simple verities:
– unhurry
– no ideas but in things
– music as meaning
– small epiphanies.

Here at Mesti, where livestock
stamped and bred,
I hear the old oaks bellowing,
carols in the horsetail falls.
A single violet fixes me
with her burning eye.

Swallows loop the loop
and shave the chalets at my feet
while wadges, scraps and tatters
lift from the valley.
Soon the high slopes wear bright patches,
petals of sunlight, early evening gifts,
– and in these snatches
I begin to sing.

Felix Mendelssohn visited Mesti, above Wengen in 1846 and painted there.

CHOUGH STRAYS SOUTH

Damask's hiss. The clinking of little
glasses no taller than my beak;

tawny-eyed kittens in baked courtyards,
burrowing and sucking, and young girls

larking down marbled passages,
skipping morning school; dance-lines

of palm-trees practising curtsies,
the sips and kisses of dazed water.

All this and the sounds lamb-clouds
do not make. A buttercup moon.

Even gulls sweet-talking, untuned
to my indigo, angry-mouthed sea.

What would I not do… I'd loop the loop
for one chill updraught, a single yelp.

ELIZABETH FRINK: 'ICARUS'

Not skedaddling. Not screaming. No,
not yet.
        He's still intent
on negotiation, on steering some way down
from such high hope and first rapture.
His mask is set – eyes marbled,
tongue sticking out, shoulders
hunched. The rudders of his pale arms
dangle like crossed claws.
At his back pink flames lick,
not yet peeling it.
                Look at the sweep
of his half-gathered hair, still oily,
still rising, like a black wing.

ATTRACTION WATER

i.m. Beth Siemon

Untrue. How can you go nowhere
when you go, a deadweight freighted
with whatever you hoped and failed to do?

Walk me down to the plank-bridge again.
Cross into that otherworld, and at once
you know the truth of it: those golden roses
embracing their canker, the square of new potatoes,
all those little shrines singing rebirth…

Follow the marl-path beside that stream
so swift with silver tildes and cedillas,
you'll soon come to the salmon-lock.

See how the voltage, unstoppable
as time, charges over the rough stone steps
and drops seething into dark pools?
Half-a-lifetime away, salmon smell it:
the sweet waters of their own beginning.

Wait now. Watch for one contrary movement,
one dream-shape summoning all its strength:
against the slipstream one life leaping.

The Mountains of Norfolk (2011)

IN THE WINDOW-SEAT

Because of the knot and Soutine swerve in the grain of this pale oak;
the slim plank's wide hips, its fit and quiet sheen;
because of its ancient wounds;
and all the veins in the greenstone, and the notch gouged in one corner;
because of the warbled panes which cannot see straight;
because of the hot eyes of the marigolds;
the rising trot of the horseman who never draws closer and never goes away;
and the moat that corrugates and comes out in goose-bumps;
because, hearing, you cannot be heard; and, seeing, you cannot be seen:

I believe that, after a long courtship, with customary decorum;
still too shy to be at ease, at the start of a suffocating afternoon;
and in haste, with lace still wrapped around one ankle, trousers half-dropped;
I believe that young and delirious, wistful, seasoned, culpable;
padding out this bay with pillows and bolsters;
fingertips sliding from skin to pane, digging into the soft cames of this
  latticed window;
in this sweet compartment;
I believe that fruitful, and with disastrous consequences, and with no obvious
  consequence at all;

as you;
as you and I;
on this common board between cradle and coffin;
first with your legs dangling over the side like a puppet's;
puffing your lower lip, cockleshelling your eyes;
and then; at long last with a long sigh;
small silver heels wedged against the riddled beam;
while the moat still dreams, thick and green, and ring-doves moan.

Because here a dragonfly settles on my right shoulder, not quite unafraid;
I believe;
as wraps of mist rise, and it is clammy evening.

OCEAN PATHS

I am crossing an ocean for you

and by whatever route and means I go,
direct or long and stopping, quick, slow,
the crossing will be slow.

I should have expected it.
A boy, I took short cuts into cul-de-sacs and deep water
and, a young man, I thought matter no match for will;
I still half-hope for the quick fix.

On the tossing northern route blue helmets howl,
the mother whirlpool grinds men's bones to salt,
and arsy-versy corkscrews twist people up and out beyond gravity.
The southern way's no better; it undermines all resolution.
Mist whitens your pupils and oozes into your brain,
it assails each cell with soft self-doubt.

Onward! Back! Sideways! On!
Voices of air and ocean swill and hammer
until you know only you cannot distinguish them.

I am crossing an ocean for you
and there is no easy way to cross an ocean
the way you cross a kitchen, a lawn, a leaping hill.
I must risk the risk I will not reach you.
B-bubbub! B-bubbub!
My old heart keeps singing in triple time.

Before I am finished, I may be a good Lutheran…
Flushed and gagging,
I will insist I want nothing easy,
nothing worthwhile comes easy,
Lord! Could be I will learn to suffer gladly.

But this way or that, you still prove me,
and guided by homing lights
transmitting their warnings and far-reaching promises,
by degrees I find myself
astonished by love.

YEARLINGS

for Nigel and Sue Cox

Sleep in a heap through the heat of the day.
They prick their ears at dusk, gangling rise,
tear off and jam on the brakes
halfway out across Two Furlong field.
Ranged in a horseshoe, they stamp and huff
and uproot the plump May grass, forgetting
quite what brought them here to begin with.
Youth's so quick. Nothing troubles them
for much more than a minute, nothing
escapes them. The moment one sheep
squeals next door, they're on their way again,
craning their lean necks right over
the hawthorn hedge to inspect the reason.
All evening they're on the go, white blazes
whiter in the gloom, racing to and fro,
quartering the field with their questions.
Very late, there's a light-show and,
catching each other's almost-terror,
they career along the foaming hedge
to the far corner ribbed with barbed wire.
So soft-eyed. So mystified.
They are languid, edgy, elegant
and, after midnight, grow so remote:
vague clouds crossing inside the skull,
shadows of something far off, long gone,
we would have done better not to have lost.

HARE

Hare knows green road and quiet lane,
hare knows well-beaten track
are best byways there and back
though her headlamps are set crooked.

> *Cat-of-the-wood and cabbage-patch stag,*
> *squat-in-the-hedge and frisker.*

Advances within herself at a slow lollop.
Stops to sniff the brisk northeasterly,
stiffens, pricks her pantomime ears,
makes off at a fair fine wallop.

> *Sit-still and shiver-maker,*
> *snuffer, twitching whisker.*
> *White spot and lie-low-by-the-dyke,*
> *boxer, little busker.*

Senses me, believes in me
– everything I and my kind can become.
With pad-scratch, sideways skelter
vanishes into long grass, fields almost golden.

> *Wide-eye, wall-eye,*
> *witch, dew-tracker, trickster.*

Except she's never anywhere else
but only where I fail to see
and just when I do not know:
at my elbow always, wherever she is.

THE PATIENT WIFE

Green dawn. That plane in my Summer Courtyard
with parakeets shrieking among her cool hands
has entwined her tall companion with gossamer,
her spiders have spun high-wire crossings,
thousands of silken strands, dewy and shining,
much more strong and supple than they appear.

He is her guardian. He overshadows her.
She's well-used to all his airs and heartaches,
his limb-secrets on long nocturnal journeys
lit by glow-worms. She is his sweet binding,
his seeress, undulant. He is her lattice,
her swoosh of laughter. Her column of tears.

I can see how she is spinning him home
from wherever he absconded last night
which she feels not the least need to know.
And he can see how she is playing him
with her weaving and waving, her enticements,
and I believe she believes he is glad of it.

HAMMERSHØI

Where there is brightness, it's always beyond,
on the other side of the wide window
– and so, by inference, before or after,
anyhow elsewhere. She waved her wand
and banished it all a long time ago.

A long time, is it? She scarcely knows.
To and fro she rocks, to and fro,
waiting while silence advances on us
and we see what she sees indoors
and out, stealthy as falling snow.

Where's that pin? She was holding it between
her bony fingers just a moment ago.

THE MOUNTAINS OF NORFOLK

in praise of sugar beet

Monstrous clamps of the great unwashed!
Grubby little Audens, dwarf-hippopotami
of the green kingdom. Each one's the sum
of its own prehistory. They smell rank already,
not like rotten trout glowing in the dark
but rubbish we forgot to chuck out yesterday.
Talk about the mountains of Norfolk...

Chalky cephalopods, their suckers and tubers
thick as penises. Grizzled old groutheads,
some scalped or shorn like combatants,
some with bristles wound round their waists.
Warty misshapen tubs, this with several snouts,
that the hooded eye of a giant tortoise.
Here's a head with the grin of a gaping shark.

Not one of them has aged beautifully.
They're like foetuses cropped from milky wombs
unformed or malformed. Boxing gloves
with knobs on. Very much more heavy
then they can possibly be. Horny, lacerated,
inescapably coarse. Not one has ever
dreamed a wild dream or seen an angel.

These thousands of stubborn brothers,
pitted, pocked and jaundiced, on a dark night
you might want to avoid them, all hunkered down
against the roaring body-snatchers.
Soon the bubbling pyre. Soon the sickly pall.
When at last the foul shall be beautiful,
and they too become authors of sweetness.

AT THE JOCH

Far below
they kicked at muddy papadums
and their doe-eyed children scrunched
and balled and hurled them, squealing.
They shivered at the indigo
overhanging them, and quaked
at the violent bellow-and-growl
they heard moments too late to witness
the avalanche. They have submitted
to layers of unknowing
and raised their eyes
to one sunstruck pitch, unbearably bright.
But nothing has prepared them for this.
Here on a slatted deck above the silent world
they stand about in shining mist,
raise their arms, bend back slender wrists,
cup their hands as lotuses,
like supplicants awaiting entry to heaven.
And now they cry sweet soft cries,
smile blissful smiles.
Turning to each other, they murmur, murmur
as very little pieces of white sky,
thousands and thousands, drift down
and touch them – their noses, lips
and eyelids, their fingertips –
gifts of clean water and quick light,
glistening white crocus,
six-pointed stars.

CHUNTERING

You're always chuntering. While you propel
yourself around your kitchenette, debating
which snack next; while you're inspecting
the myriad channels, and with little
shuffling penguin steps heading fast
for the deck where you take a dim view
of the ice-blue weather. As if word
makes flesh. As if word drives your heart.

Often, your patter dovetails now with then,
and your mnemonics summon companions:
yesterday's nurse, cautioning you not to fall,
not to fall, and the state trooper warning
'youths will shoot you as soon as look at you'.
Also Pastor Nelson, God's narrow spokesman
– but above all your pit-prop, wise and warm,
icebound for two years now at Fort Snelling.

Several times each day you begin to giggle.
You giggle and gasp, and then announce
you really don't know why. Because you've seen
it all; because whatever's not unbearable
has become absurd. Fortified by small
essential household wonders, and rosy,
unshakeable in your faith, you laugh
until tears stream down your crumpled cheeks.

BREATHLESS

The barn owl holds our breath,

– contemplatives peaceful
as lily-pads, having learned
to bottom out and fathom the world,

transformed now into pilgrims,
stricken almost by this first sight
of the one we've longed to see.

In this easterly bluster he balances
on a stanchion, perfectly aware
we're observing him ignoring us.

With vast unhurried wing-sweeps
he rises silent above himself,
hangs on nothing, sizes everything.

All his days a readying for this
moment when he gathers, swells,
swoops behind the hawthorn hedge

and gives us back, breathless.

RISING

And on all sides
always
lie the fields
of flint
– another million
surfacing
each night
from the chalky soil,
keen light
knapping them,
oatmeal,
grey-green, ghostlike
as waves breaking.
Flashing
dragon's teeth
of these salt-acres
where first
shall be last,
while hidden
beneath the last
of the last
sings our song
always,
shines our gold torque,
turns the key
to our hill-house
of green
words rising.

HUBBUB

> *for all the hubbub and the blather,*
> *and the tyranny of choice,*

which way from babeldom
to syllables of sound
– each tone of the heart,
and the brain inch-inching
along the path of reason?

> *for all the ease and do-as-you-please,*
> *the pick-and-mix smile and voice*

which way from cradle and breast
to the sheer crossing-place,
the battleground
wound in dark veils,
home of the hard-won?

> *for all the creeds and dusty screeds,*
> *the hand-me-down and the decreed*

which way, like a novice
eager to unlearn,
from will to willing
and that shining emptiness,
the cloud of unknowing?

> *for all our doubt and self-doubt,*
> *our seasons of drought*

which way from yesterday and tomorrow,
to one song
wild and soaring,
still unsatisfied,
here, now and for ever?

> *for all the hubbub and the blather,*
> *for all the ease and do-as-you-please,*
> *for all the creeds and dusty screeds,*
> *for all our doubt and self-doubt*

one song wild and soaring,
here now, now and for ever

The Breaking Hour (2015)

BOYHOOD

1

Let me begin again.

No, not embedded in the womb
but with this boy in sensible grey shorts
the way he walks no distance
between actual and numinous.

So eager, so open-eyed

so involved with story
but in Chesterton's white light
unbothered by what was or will be,
mythology, metaphor.

Let him recover me.

2

Above me the chalk cross soared
from our doorstep to heaven.
I knew it always had,
and always would.

Below me the train steaming
from where to where across the blue Vale
coughed and paused
at Monks Risborough and Whiteleaf Halt.

Still so uncurious,
yet so soon to set out
wyde in this world wondres to here.

3

'Do you want to remember
here and now?'

In my bath I squirmed round.
'What do you mean? How?'

'By deciding to. By wanting to so much
there's nothing in your head, your heart
but this steamed-up room,
look, this laundry-box, your yellow towel,
you, me, these words…'

I stood up and dried myself, properly.
Mindful, I walked out of Eden.

TRANSLATIONS

for Dom and Kas

Scan

As when some steepling wave
seems arrested, or cumuli
draw close, couple and configure,
we glimpse this dream made flesh,
half-smiling, left hand raised.
And each of us comes face to face
with innocence, manifest,
ineffable unearthly bliss
before we compromise it.

Before the Breaking Hour

Love-knot, dovetail, harvest bow:
they've waited all their lives for you
and wish you everything they want.
Their sit-at-home, their rope-dancer,
their hyphen and fuse and chord:
now, before the breaking hour,
vital image, simplifying word.

Cradle

Not woven from purple rushes
and, daubed with slime and pitch,
left to bob among flags.
Not lined with watercolour silks
– gifts of the Good Fairies.
Nothing less than this soft rain
so still through the watches,
each sweet drop giving voice
to earth and grass, leaf, roof,
pane, and yes, whatsoever is.

COMMUNION

No, I never commune with my ancestors
before breakfast. But the roneo'd foolscap
pages of *Lore and Legend of Flintshire,*
musty yet tart, opened the creaking door
to my father's study; and this afternoon,
while rummaging for two-inch nails
in a cigar-box stuffed with nothing but screws,
I encountered my grandfather Frank
gazing at me over his half-moons,
beginning a homily. At certain times
my younger son does look uncommonly
like him. And just now I'm well aware
of a whole blood-company of crooks,
antiquarians, ministers and warriors
standing behind me, awaiting the firstborn
and hardwon, all of them silent, all attentive.

MIRIAM

for my first grandchild, born on 16th August 2012

I have entered the garden of superstition
where it is unwise to gaze at moon jellyfish
or the undersides of toadstools
and a scuff on the bracelet bearing your name
may be no less a portent
than a crack in the teacup or temple.

Fairy godmothers and Fortune herself
are not so much inevitable as invited.
I am in league with prime numbers,
hagstones and anagrams – even the lottery –
and potter about, smelling lavender.
I consort only with whatever is propitious.

Each day I am learning more
about longing and the longed for,
attending to my Hebrew.
I have met your half-sisters,
Maria and Mariam, Minnie, Maire,
and I kneel before the Virgin.

Etymology has its limitations.
Your name like all names grows in sound:
the humming of bees, vowels cheeping,
and that capricious r, rolled in the throat
or butterfly light, fluttering on the tip
of the tongue. That's the sum of it.

TRESPASSES

for Sally, my sister

Often we inspected our father's beds,
each ruled with drills straight as staves,

our mother's rockery stitched with Alpines
airlifted home, wrapped in damp muslin,

but it was the gooseberries behind the old shed
claimed us and blood-blushed our wrists.

Between two rows we scooped our hidey-hole
and topped and tailed with our thumb-nails,

and that was where we welcomed Bruce
with open arms after the massacre.

He planted his victims like a regular gardener
only to turn his back and ignore them,

but later suffered a Buff Orpington
around his bull neck by way of punishment.

'He'll never do it again. He won't, will you?'
Bruce whisked his tail, he rapped it,

his dark eyes gleamed, and on our knees
beside our bunk three times we murmured

the Lord's Prayer, then absolved him
in the blue hour and slipped his lead.

Silent as death, we slunk away,
past the shed, past the morgue,

then tore up Whiteleaf Hill, rejoicing.

WATER-SPIRIT

Wimblington is where you fell out of the sky
not at first like a sweet shower on a changeable day.
I'm thinking of the way like a shining spear or javelin
a waterfall can spout quite clear of a cliff, her force
for a moment little less than gravity, before she arcs
above a valley, graceful and loosening, and drifts
to the supple floor, an umbrella golden, many-coloured.
Water-spirit, my own daughter, rising, riding,
I see you falling, falling and laughing. Elementary.

KIM'S GAME: FIRST VARIATION

Begin with a dozen items, their order determined
only by pulse and music. The sound of night-rain,
very softly falling. The smell of chloroform,
and a chess-set fashioned from ivory and light.
That secret I can never share, and the stench
of my own fear. The high jinks of the first swallow.
A Liberty handkerchief (*circa* 1976),
and the aroma of wild strawberries. The scent
of a baby. Crunch-crunch of snow underfoot.
That fatal first kiss… Well, I'm keeping one
to myself for the moment. This is my game now.

I knew what was to come after the cake
and candles and the snaps with the Brownie:
that dreadful covered tray… My throat grew dry.
So why am I still competing, and with whom
(eg. the Grim Reaper, Dr Alzheimer, no-one)?
Gut has guided me, and I see all five senses
are represented, though I've this sense sometimes
of something beyond sense. No ideas but
in things, true, but in things not only presences,
absences too. Please go back to the beginning.
Would you care to adopt any of my items?

PASSAGES

Che faro...

Not the flap-flap and boom of a marquee
or the raucous joy of wild geese returning,
not leaf-scrape and rattle or some hailer
broadcasting from other worlds,
not even a single insistent fly
weaving around a clammy wrist...

*

In the chill enclosure – its only sound
no-sound, the pressure of it,
wanting even the breath and beat of being –
white mist lifted, dipped,
and the wraiths listened...

*

When Orpheus played and sang
he gave them back their time,
gave them memory...

*

And that he sang as he did,
standing where the passage widened
and admitted a shaft of pale daylight,
as if for the first time he understood
how he must find in grief growth
and whatever's fruitful:
he was so whole-hearted,
so generous, and that only made
his desolation more unbearable...

LIFELINES

Grey-green thunderhead. So tell me,
who scrapped it because of this fissure?
A lookalike with a stubborn jaw, high cheekbones
and an engaging chuckle?

This lip of a Samian dish,
did it slip through the fingers of some Norfolk lass
harassed and ravished by a Dalmatian horseman
in his cups?

And this dividing-bowl; this dandy;
this slim-hipped girl; this neck of a nacreous bottle;
this little finger...

Between outrageous thistles
and patches of vetch, yellow-and-purple, beneath
our springing soles, an inch deep, a yard,
never much more than that, they're all so much
closer than we think.

Closer and warmer,
immune to illness, scornful of the shining edge,
lying in wait like rolling fairground pennies,
lodged across the lines between who they were
and might have been.

Yes, we squinted
at the same sun and were assailed
by the same bitter squalls. Bleached
by salt, we lived within earshot
of the same ocean.

But who were they,
these men and women with their litters of children
and scrawny herds of animals,
on their way between worlds,
and how are we to understand them?
What did they mean?

This pierced coin,
is it an affirmation of Empire,
a talisman, a love token, or simply
the difference between a full stomach
and going to bed hungry?

Birth and hope,
maddening passion, each of our stepping-stones
attended by rituals, as we hasten
towards the Four Last Things:
the very abstracts that unite us
separate us.

And yet, sometimes
– times between times – when the fret
lifts and the world grows wholly wonderful,
we believe for a moment that we've levelled
our gaze and are singing in unison,

and only our own doubt
and sense of difference dates us.
Look! They have not gone away.
Not one of them. It is we who leave them;
and now all we can do is love and grieve them.

Warham Camp and Branodunum

IN HAGIA SOPHIA

1 Varangian Mercenary

What if there's no afterlife, least not
for the likes of me, and after death
nothing but afterdeath? So what!

Pff! I'm pickled as a herring.
Since when did the dead ever go away?
We live in the presence of our ancestors.

Soon enough she'll get the better
of my rotten body – that's up to fate –
but I'll not have Time outstrip me.

Here now. On this shining ledge
I'll score my runes and rub blood into them.
That I am. That once upon a time I was.

2 Enrico Dandolo's Tombstone

Blind magician, stop-at-nothing boss,
maestro of the Adriatic. You caustic
tongue-twister, you ancient extractor,
levelled at last on this disputed ground
– crosses and candles, six-lobed coronas –
underfoot at the feet of your only Master
and the flashing mosaic you never saw.

Byzantium's sons dismembered you,
and her avenging daughters threw
their mongrels your old bones.
Today and yesterday and tomorrow...
Down, down again, stammering down
from the dark-eyed dome: feather-flames
still writhing over your unquiet tomb.

THE ROSES OF CAMON

in memory of Helen Barber

Afin que vif et mort ton corps ne soit que roses

Who was she, Madame Alfred Carrière?
Aromatic as linen newly pressed,
Sprinkled with citrus. Zéphirine Drouhin,
So pink and pretty and small, so intense?
And Madame Isaac Pereire? Musky.
Almost her own dish of pot-pourri.
Yolande d'Aragon? Where are they now?
Gone to ground, all of them, in this bitter season.
New Dawn and Buff Beauty, Blossom,
Violette, Crimson Glory… they sound
Like top flight fillies, cheek by jowl
With poet and cardinal in these narrow beds.
Ah, dear one, *Allons voir si la rose*
Que ce matin avoit desclose
Sa robe de pourpre au Soleil,
A point perdu ceste vesprée
Les plis de sa robe pourprée
Et son teint au vostre pareil.

1825! 1840. '78… '80… 1895.
Here they are, this gathering, whose donors
Preferred circling seasons to the perpetual,
Freezing stars, avenues of planes or poplars,
Or cobbled streets in Old Towns.
Look! Loved ones, heroes and heroines,
Muses, memorials, imports, late arrivals,
Even descendants of the hardy stock
Farmers planted one thousand years ago
To gauge the health of their hillside vines –
Bare roots jostling beside the river,
All spit-and-hurtle, and the leaping railway bridge.
Las, voyez comme en peu d'espace
Ah, dear one, *elle a dessus la place*

Las! las ses beautez laissé cheoir!
Not for you the exotic (say, King of Siam)
Or the *Almanach de Gotha* (Crown Princess Margareta)
Or lush Rhapsody in Blue. Not the winged one
Or the wimpled, blurred with her own incense,
Not even the improbable Threepenny Bit.
Your favourite was the single Cocktail,
Village cousin of the ramping Dog Rose.
True, five or six blooms in each cluster
(Unlike you, an only child), but each of them
So open-faced, so independent.
Upright. Very bright. Yellow and red
And a stamen creamy, deepening to apricot.

You said she was long-lasting and unblinking,
And I thought of you as unafraid, a truth-teller.
Questioning, challenging, always persistent.
You said yes, she was tough-minded.
You said she was prickly, but quite attractive
To bees. Hostile, however, to drones, I supposed.
Strong willed, I thought. Seldom in doubt.
But when you smiled and slightly trembled
I surmised you were laughing at yourself.

How bedded you were in your Suffolk acres,
Affirming your husband and your home,
The cornucopia in your own garden.
With the sheaf of your hair loosely tied
In a golden bun or a harvest bow, you'd arrive
On our doorstep with an overflowing basket.
O vrayment marâtre Nature,
Puis qu'une telle fleur ne dure
Que du matin jusques au soir!

Your eye was so sharp. I doubt you ever
Missed a cedilla or circumflex.
Reading... assessing... corresponding
(Your round hand open, that of a young girl)...
You were never a woman so busy with omens
Or the numinous that you failed
To be curious about whatever is:
Age, fabric, detail, sound, tone, design.

White Grootendorst and Renaissance,
Christoph Colomb, Baron Girod de l'Ain
(A true dandy, crimson with a white rim):
In the little courtyards and up flaking walls,
Around two rickety chairs and the drinking table,
– In the stillness of the village and the cloister,
Imperturbable, of l'Abbaye-Château,
All the roses of Camon are rising again.
Belle Hélène de citron et de miel,
They will breathe, breathe and quiver.
In their summer season they will nod and incline.
Ah, dear one, we will remember you.

IN ST. EMMERAM-KIRCHE

What if this were all true?

Just a couple of beats before the first bar of Opus 21 (C major), Row G
  of the burghers assembled beneath the gold-and-white unsmilingly make
  room for a petite blonde Minnesotan.

Within touching distance, her old husband sits behind a powder-blue pillar.
  He removes his shoes. He presses his soles against the cool tiles.

He's standing close, the old man thinks.

Godfather Death.

Very close.

He is standing between us.

What nonsense, thinks the old man. Godfather Death lives nowhere but
  within each one of us.

But then he recalls bargains brokered with Death, deals enabling men and
  women to remain a little longer on sweet earth.

They're in the air, he thinks, these stories. The east wind blows them in
  from Bohemia. I do not disbelieve them.

The first movement of the first symphony is by now well underway.

Godfather Death is standing so close, the old man thinks.

He turns and smiles at his wife. He's remembering the way only last evening,
  only last evening, the daisies shone silver beneath her feet.

The petite blond Minnesotan reaches out, very firmly she grasps her old
  husband's outstretched hand.

At bar 92 (as it later transpires) a grizzled citizen in Row E coughs. He
  coughs and gargles. He gargles and he slumps.

Behind him, the burghers and their wives stiffen, and do their very best not to show they have noticed.

She would not go, the old man thinks, sitting behind his powder-blue pillar.

She would not let me go.

Not yet, no.

What was the bargain?

The old man keeps the beat. With his right forefinger, he gently taps his right kneecap.

Regensburg

ON COMING SECOND

Second fiddle, second best, second rate.
Runner-up: the word itself's an also-ran.

When my mother's father's grandfather
rode third in the Aylesbury Steeplechase
with 'its rattling good jump, 18 feet
of naked water', his neighbours lifted him
on their shoulders, they tossed him
halfway to heaven.
             And to finish fourth
in track or field – out of the medals,
out of the money – is halfway
between exasperation and heartbreak.
Even fifth is very far from ignominious,
while to come last has a certain distinction.
La lanterne rouge, the wooden spoon.
On the green baize after mock O-levels:
GERMAN. CROSSLEY-HOLLAND, K. 3%.
And beneath it, typed in scarlet capitals:
ADVISED NOT TO SIT EXAM.
             Once you determine
your offspring's no budding Victor Ludorum,
please advocate a completely different tack:
bobbing apples, say, or vowing to enter
the record book with matchbox tops,
or else pursuing the strictly non-competitive:
– a study of natterjack toads in Cumbria,
compound nouns in contemporary verse,
something astral or wholly conjectural.

'Tough! Well tried! Better luck next time!'
I see those damp, lower lips protruding, those
discreet tweed jackets.
             It's not winning
that matters. Not much. It's not failing.
Second string, second gear, second class!
Runner-up: the word itself's an also-ran.

'Second?' my wife drawls. 'Nothing better.
That's what any proper Lutheran prays for.'

SEPTEMBER

1

Sprays of elderberries spilling
out of hedge-windows, pretty not indecorous,
blatant hips, Byzantine eyes
deep-set and misty, these and a copia
of ripe blackberries flanked by tall nettles,
each papula plump and glistening.

Content and consummate, late fruit
are always now-or-neverish.

Coming and going, almost blazing sun
hurries goldfinches to the spilling seeds
of thistle and lavender, and here,
couched amongst ragged, downy heads
stands this perfect clock, a single one,
that has forgotten to tell the time.

2

Waking me, circling the grey horizon,
Lakenheath thunder I mistake at first
for something natural. Rain as fine
as stitching, petit point, silk samplers.
Our garden neither accepts nor rejects it
– blades, petals, leaves all look glassy.

Now, wings thrashing in the thicket!
Piteous piping. Slight scrape of my sandals.

No ambition, no further expectation:
each hour is whey-faced, scarcely
rising. Not even a thimbleful of wind.
Caught in her mauve and pewter
pleats, the garden is listening to herself,
beginning the work of her own grieving.

WHAT SHE PROMISES

As usual
and almost daily as bread
books weigh in,
hundreds of thousands millions
of characters
and silences.

If not from the shop
they slip or squeeze
through the sprung flap
drop and slide on their bottoms
across the honeyed tiles.
Some are involved in a small ceremony
some are blessings banes or bores
but each one uncommon
and singular evidence
even the most trifling.

Matter of the spirit,
surroundings, stomach,
home-grown and far-flung:
after the first quick inspection
– font, weight of paper,
self-effacing stitching
or odourless glue,
how the leaves rustle,
the untold ways books mean –
we set them all aside.
In wonky piles
each waits her turn
some rising
some sinking
as seasons pass
destined always to lie low.

Here's one still pristine
in her soapy cellophane.
Ah! Short or long her time
is bound to come.

After some grievous loss,
or locked in loneliness,
we'll unwrap her promises
– this charm waiting to console
even to heal us,
the secret of laughter.

A QUIET MIND

Disembarrassed of all obligations,
the little rituals, dozens of chores
I require and even cherish,
well away from that lofty place
where hunks of chalk, knapped flint
and pale pink brick make subtle harmonies,

and light flooding from four quarters
quickens the colours of invigoration,
quietens the tones of contemplation;
where, through the study's double door,
I can hear women's voices dovetailing
in the kitchen, the old kettle shushing,

yet sit at the desk rebuked for knowing all of it
not as it is but for what I'm making of it
– a cell, a shield where I leave
the spirit like mud on the doorstep
and there's always something more pressing
than to sit and dream and wait and write:

I crouch at the hearth of your Suffolk house
well within earshot of the German Ocean
but for the huge throat gulping and roaring
and the howitzer of a north-easterly
hurling pellets of hail and snow,
coldest of corn, across the tiled courtyard.

The other rooms are pantry-chill, cellar-chill,
heavy-curtained inside, snow-curtained outside,
but here the heart is simmering with half-said
and unsaid because there's no need to say,
the cracking of vast, slow-burning plane logs,
laughter, the antiphon of old friendship.
One by one I start to jettison dog-eared files:
CURRENT, ACTION, URGENT, HERE AND NOW.
I call to postpone long-arranged meetings,
then make an appointment for a heart
out of tune. I write postcards to bright teenagers,
and order mulch for the wakening beds.

George Crabbe crabbed here, Quilter composed,
Boyd hoisted his canvas, Hill located a peacock.
Here on this cusp of a sandy peninsula
lay gold and garnets in the graves of Wuffings,
and the scop sang: *Relish every thing!*
Make good use of each and every thing!

The lion on your sooty fire-back
opens his jaws; lying flat, the shining bellows sigh.
John Ogilby's on his way from London to Yarmouth
(122 miles, 5 furlongs). Even Guinevere escapes
her unending, stricken dream... What's the point
of memory if not to help resolve us?

Until once again I begin to link words
and discover a story – very far from certain
which way forward, knowing only the gift
is mine to fashion and give what's due back:
come the bright morning when I purr north,
unhurrying, quick to myself again.

THE SYRIAN GODDESS

Sea-monsters, she's seen her fair share of those
– many more than cartographers
fossicking in reading rooms
and poring over unwieldy maps,
their borders crowded with tritons and sea-pigs
and other horrid crossbreeds.

She has even ridden on Leviathan,
he who *maketh the deep to boil like a pot*
and a path to shine after him.

But this soft skywater
gathered in the scallops of rocks above the tideline,
soured already,
gone yellow-green and unholy,
and the ocean itself,
oleaginous and sluggish and stinking...

Atargatis lifts her eyes
and stares at herself
throttled between clouds, charcoal, indigo.
She waits for her hour to come
and her heart races,
she thrashes her tail.

Before dawn the sky splits open
and again the dark stars hiss. They whistle and they scream.
They begin to explode.

Mortal and ragged,
from her own children her children shield their eyes.
They kneel and burrow
and stumble through the wreckage.

At the crossing-place, the goddess weeps; she weeps.
Tears of clearest quartz, tears of blood.
She stoops and catches water
in the cup of her hands. She cradles it.

ON THE COCKLE-PATH

It's a kind of steeplechase.
                              A deep black eye
awaits and the young step straight into it
– a ritual anointing. 'Iodine!'
grandfather says. ' Prophylactic.'
Also, well-nigh indissoluble.
Locals sidestep it, and now and then
some furriner cracks a femur
or tibia.
          Next, skin-rasping sea-blite
and dozens of pulks tiled with mud mosaic,
Byzantine streams in winding canyons,
the tumbledown bridge decorated
with badges of burned orange lichen.
Nothing is ever easy on the saltmarsh.

A small pool clear as a cloud-window,
fringed with thrift – that's where they're hanging.
Half-in, half-out: just testing the water.
Copper and caramel, blonde, chestnut,
their long hair's unleashed and interwoven
with green strings. Seaweed shoulder straps.
Green satin drapes over their lean limbs,
it slips between their fingertips.
                                    To be mobbed
by mermaids, and favoured with a knob
of sea-lavender, mauve, almost musty.
Whimsical? Wistful? By no means.

These are apprentices, spellbound by boy bands
and Jessie J, up to their necks
in social networking. Two play the guitar,
unaware their combs are plectra.
One has grade VI (harp) with distinction,
another's been to Copenhagen. Of course
they know mermaids and seal-women are magical,
but allow Sheila Disney with her moustache
and webbed feet (she taught them to swim)

may have been the last child of a seal-family.
As for them… Atta-who? Atargatis…
They shrug their tanned shoulders.
                                    They've heard
they can raise storms but not how or why.

They're not freighted with tales or harsh truths
and have yet to learn how their kind kidnapped
poor Hylas.
                    They paint their nails
viridian, and dream boys will fall for them,
but don't mean to wound them or eat them alive,
only to swamp them in their unblinking pools.

They chant as they toss their tears,
but keep dropping them.
                                    Tidal, that's what they are,
lucent, already welling, waves-in-the-gathering.
Saltwaters make and pull around them,
chime and chuckle, and engage with them.

GIRL WITH HAWK

Harebells, scabious, foxglove,
swaying grasses:
she was so slender, so light on her feet,
assembled almost
from Pennine flowers,
but then that's how they sometimes are,
the really tough ones.

On the mica track below Odin's Mine
she stopped and accosted us
and, handsome and dusky,
her Harris hawk
knife-eyed me:
Each life feeds my life
unless she denies me.

'He flew off. Ignored me.
Two miles out across Edale.
I've had one adventure today, I can tell you.'
And then: 'A tiny transistor on his left leg.
He was still hungry
and, praise be, I'd got a few scraps left.'

'His manna,' I volunteered.
'My salvation!
Just bits and bobs, but he's not picky.
My last boyfriend!'
Chestnut and charcoal stripes.
Glaring at me staring at him
jouncing on her right wrist.

'Just joking!'
She gave me such a tearing look
the curious sheep backed off
and turned their butts towards us.
'Been up Mother Hill, then? Seen the earthworks?
They used to eat them, their enemies, they did.
Come on boy! Come on, darling!'

FLEDGLING MAYBE, MAYBE WINGED

for Polly Ionides

Charged with our two-minded Mother Tongue
garnished with adoptions, adaptations
and choice pickings from the lexicon,
unrestricted by academicians and nervous ministers…
Wolf and chaste, corn and blood and mourning:
we apportion each full moon her proper name
and the rogue blue does not phase us, and yet
for her winged sister, ethereal fledgling
– windstorms, moonstorms, nothing but dissent.

Black, and Finder's, and Secret, and Spinner's
drawing and twisting us towards our own
destinies: while rock-jawed dogmatists
lock horns with witches and worshippers,
this almost disembodied shape, little more
than the idea of one, runs ahead of herself again
through hurtling clouds, never to be caught
except in some sky-net quivering
with kennings, stars and shining metaphors.

SIX NORFOLK POEMS

1 Words

Go back at last to the lost beginning
and you will find them waiting not hidden
strewn among pink stars on the saltmarsh
in shallow scrapes beside the speckled eggs
of the little divebombers and shocking
as drops of blood on the shingle rashes.

In this place you've always known and thought
you knew – beyond the Nod, no further than Missel,
all bindweed bells now, blite, blue-green holly:
pick up your old pointer beneath this torrent
of fervent light, ready yourself again
to winnow and to pitch, and prick out.

2 Nelson Country

Because this is my childhood staithe?
A matter of identity? Consolation?

I no longer know why I come back
but know this flux is crucial as breathing
and this place so demanding, sometimes harsh
(treacly mud, flint-grey creeks, oozing marsh)
it expects me. It brings me to book.

Each man must do all he can do
and he must say all he can say. Amen.

3 These Things

The coast road was closed, the death-marsh deserted,
strewn with magazines, lights, twisted metal,
    and on the foreshore 1000 spirits of the dead
    gathered then rose in missing man formation.
In sunlight the F-15s aimed far inland, heading
for the rituals and tears at Lakenheath

while the wild geese flew far out, protesting,
  high over wave-beat and wind-blather.
Ashen in the mourning wind, banded together.
  Flap and palaver, fury and feather.
'These things we do that others may live.'
  Helpless, and facing even worse weather.

4 Clarification

Sea-coal his wide eyes
burning with blue flames.

Half the night he dances
on his own casts and carbuncles
and climbs far above his station.

Singing it and springing it.
Making it.
No bounds.

At dawn, he rises
through light levels
as bubbles rise.

He almost clarifies

and his see-through shrimps scoot
among leftovers: scurf, froth, weed.

5 Wintering Grounds

They're back!
              Back from the capes
of Greenland, and Spitzbergen, Iceland,
their ranks ragged, frosty-grey arrowheads
and groups of outliers in wavering lines.
What is it so tugs at the heart?
Sheer wonder it has happened again
– the same geese, these same acres –
and on our doorsteps,
the sudden surge of wild longings?

Is it their conversation, so scratchy, terse,
insisting nothing is easy on earth?
Their fierce delight, rounding on a field
of waste potatoes, barley stubble –
or our own, knowing good times lie ahead?

    6 Creation Light

Due north…

ignites the horse-chestnut's topmost candle
dances on the saltmarsh with will-o'-the-wykes
opens peat envelopes on the silken beach.
How many wild bees are draped on Norton
tower? Can you see tomorrow?

…veering north-easterly

Before I'm an hour older I'll skim over
the solder of the cold German Ocean
and splosh across polders shoulder to shoulder
with strapping women. This creation light!
Let me echo let me rhyme and chime

to brazen Amsterdam.

SEA-DEW

in memory of Rosemary Crossley-Holland

Open your heart to its slow roll
over – this vast spring tide driving
through the bellbuoys and mackerel shallows
from the flares of Forties and wild Viking,
at last first landing on Scolt Head.

White-caps along the foreshore are making merry.

And high on Chalk Hill the lane is milky,
wavy hedges and verges are shining
with sea-dew – foam of quickthorn, wild cherry,
nettles, cow parsley – and descants
and downpours blossoming before the dark.

PRAYER

Pillar of dust, kindled by the sun.
Shaft quicksilvered by the swimming moon.

Give me the grasp to apprehend, and
the grace to make light of my understanding.

Gravity for Beginners (2021)

SEAHENGE: A JOURNEY

for Andrew Rafferty

1 Tump

Back again! Back
and up to that oval tump above the chalk cross
to search for a thumbnail of pottery,
a single sherd.
When I launched myself into the trench beside it,
packed with crackling beech-leaves,
I believed I was an inmate of the barrow.

Commentator, diplomat, viola player, priest
– all four beached on my limitations
and quickening sense of myself.
But why did I not train to be an archaeologist?

That riddled oak lectern,
and the scarabs and beads from Ur,
a nacreous perfume bottle lifted
from some settlement south of Alexandria…
Asking, deducing, dovetailing
past and present, matter and spirit:

my heart quickens
to Whiteleaf and my childhood museum,
that shed growing into the ground,

and with one eye on the threatening sky,
one on a molehill,
I brighten at the little finds
I'm still adding to it.

2 Deadheaded

Undone, a necklace of rose lights
looping over the Chilterns
above the spring line
(no culture chooses to look down at its dead)
then on through the wilderness of this world
– the airy Downs, silly Suffolk –
each blossom radiant, fading,
deadheaded.

Sky widens, and the chain tautens.
Footfalls in the sandy soil and soggy fen,
footfalls through forests bedded
with cones and needles:
knappers and salt-panners and oyster-men,
truth-tellers, outcasts, devotees
still resting here.

Sudden gusts and bluster,
bolts of thunder, stinging rain,
and no less sudden,
wings of Chalk Hill blues again.

High over the henge and all its voices
there's a spray of lights, a cluster:
shoulder-companions on this last ridge
at the end of their long journey
– dark roses before the drop
to the baffled sea.

3 Unliving

With mommets and hodmedods
we tried to scare him away.
For a while we did.
Death flew off with his demons
and you burned brightly.

When we propped you
against the door-post
you heard your willow-daughter
comforting her daughter
who will soon be born.

You kept begging us
to call on our ancestors.
Flame-cheeks, twitch-fingers.
You kept saying the unliving
can guard the living.

   4 Shimmer

All day you waited
outside your hut,
not alone,

and murmured and warbled
last words
before you lost your breath.

You watched how the ridge
grew holy
and how the end of the evening
shimmered
the bristling fields
copper and bronze

even your own messengers
the waves of the sky
no longer mud-foul
but oyster and pearl

while sea-eagles and harriers
before their bloody work
made low passes

   5 Tree

When you came I was unborn.

No one knew your name
or where you had walked from.
'Along the living streams,' you said.

You told us there's a tree
opening over all that is

all that is
– white skull, green earth, swarming sea.
'It sings and suffers for us.
It is our always tree.'

You said when our leader dies,
each of us is turned over, each broken.
You told us to smash all the death-urns
and nick the axe-blades
to set their spirits free,
then lay him in the cradle
of an upturned tree.

'Do this,' you said,
'and he will be sky-born again.
After the fire and flood
you too will be sky-born again.'

Our grandfathers and great grandmothers
laughed they cried
and in the rush-light
they asked you many questions.

I know I would have seen you
before sunrise
up there on the lopeway
just below the ridge.

6 Altar

I closed your lids
with this right thumb.
Then we fashioned your death-cradle.
The elders and the lame
with chains of song unbroken,
and the young splashing, delving, squeezing out,
then heaping up your island,
all the men and women with their singing axes.

With honeysuckle ropes we snared the posts
and set them up in trenches side by side.
Past the hazels and alders
we hauled the huge oak-stump

with its horn roots to the bog.
We chipped all the bark
from your cradle.
>> *Your white altar.*
>> *Your shining altar.*

From where sun dies the wind blew,
tides gulped and shunted
behind our dunes for many days.
But at last we lifted you
on thick green trusses and silver wormwood
we carried you out from the dead-house.
>> *You wore flowers.*
>> *You wore flowers.*

Sun-cups, silken cottongrass,
threaded and twisted,
starlight, marsh-mallow.
Your choker wreathen sea-pink.

So gently we laid you
on the crush of chalk and clay
between the roots
of the upturned tree.
>> *Our death-baby.*
>> *Our death-baby.*

Each of us sipped three sips
of the sweet water, the sweet water
lapping you.
And I, blood of your blood,
placed your death-gifts around you.

The sea-eagles and harriers heard our cries.
They cried with us.

Then each of us sang.
I sang I felt the darkness knotting
inside you.
I sang you were the setting sun.
I sang until I closed the lids
over your eyes
with this right thumb
sky always always shone in them.

7 Crossing

Marram whipped, peat-lipped,
salt-scoured, windswept:
the earth meets the sea

and each opens to the running sky
and reflects it. Gazing across
the wash of years

we say this stark foreshore
where flux is the only constant
looks entirely fitting

as the site of a crossing-place;
and while we recognise
it's not what its makers intended

with their plans for circles and walkways
well-guarded by dunes,
and their heroic labour,

see also that time and dream
have mapped and remapped it
into another truth.

8 Tides

Of what once was
what's left will soon be gone.

Without kicking up more waves
of argument and speculation,

or putting unanswerable
philosophical questions...

Still not knowing how not to look,
and not to ask but breathe

and have my own tides reveal
what they will and when they will.

Wrynecks drum, grey plovers whistle,
and boring piddocks have their way.

Of what once was
what's left will soon be gone.

Wholly to immerse myself
wholly to find myself.

Not to search for words words
but in this place only to be.

9 Burden

Not sorry and not stricken
but of age
I'll strip my scape
to headland
          and heartland.

Let each silence
          and breath
each word-in-waiting
learn to bear a burden
weightless as eternity.

TIME'S FOOL

Ocean's always more than we can make of it,
a better metaphor than any for two-handed time.

Swashbuckle, yes, and silver spears shaking,
that's how it was at the top of the tide,

but each wave breaking grew reluctant
to sort shingle, dissolve casts, even to adjust

that scribble of froth and stringy weed,
seacoal, mermaids' purses, bottles, brattlings.

Tide on the drag (after the equipoise)
lays bare our whole expanse of days

– momentary migrants reflected in water,
skimming over the foreshore, its shallows

and snags, hidden clear-eyed pools –
and then it summons from the deep

raven Thought, cormorant Memory.
Before tide's down and out, sandflats and slakes

become teeming wordbeds, salty and lucent,
where it's time always to address time.

SACRAMENTAL

for Linda

We could commit the whole day
to this heavenly squelch
beyond the muddy paths and sour pans
cracking into soft, salt-bleached
mosaics. We'd try to match
what Latin names we remember
to the bristle-and-cocoon footing
this ocean of musty sea-lavender:

(Shadow-sweep: a marsh harrier.)
Saltmarsh grass and sea blite,
samphire twigs, almost luminous;
stands of sea purslane and red fescue.
(Taste of silt and sharp iodine.)
Here's a bone-house of sally crabs,
and a wicked witch's purse,
spikes we've never seen before…

What happens in this all but silent space,
preceding thought, inviting it,
is never simple, always changing.
An oystercatcher's *kleeep*. Sucks. Sighs.
Each sound or movement of what's hidden
signifies. Look! This shining shrimp
– leaping opal! The word on the tip
of your tongue may be sacramental.

FRENCH LEAVE

Sometimes the neap is surreptitious,
so soft so steady there's neither swill
nor suck as she slides into the muddy
staithe and lifts skiffs on their anchors,
shifting, out-eager, dreaming of searoom.

Just a jasmine smudge and a dozen
stars, a few marsh birds still conferring.
Three boys on the jetty, shoulder to shoulder.
Low voices, each daring the others.

They can hear the punch, the pound,
distant, arhythmical, and the shingle
cracking. Tide's almost on the ebb
again, they can see the red eyes
winking. The coast is quite clear.

MOCK MEDIEVAL: BRANCASTER BEACH

This lesser barbican, kin to some vast stronghold,
already looked ancient when it was young.
One face of the bastion collapsed, in fact,
while the builders were still on site,
but it boasted a redoubtable keep,
most ornately decorated, a deep moat
and, improbably, a minaret.
On its gritty haunches it sat,
scarcely less staunch than Bamburgh
or some brick-and-mortar shore fort,
facing foursquare across the German Ocean.

Clammy the dungeon and mightily constricted.
Carting and thumping and caressing,
three maidens down there with a little lad
(all four scantily clad) laboured to reinforce
the oozing walls. Full of dread and desire,
they exhorted one another with shrieks
and squeals, aware that even a short delay
was the best they could hope for.
Such innocent and willing victims
of the shining moon, the deadly god,
driven to their own destruction.

THE TIDE

On her way out, as she almost always is
this high up the muddy creek, so far
from the wailing and gleeful ocean.

What's revealed would be mostly
better hidden – stinking dregs, a midden
such as miserable Grimes wallowed in –

all but one furious inspector,
white of white, infinitely patient,
then thrusting and stabbing.

*

First light, celadon in the south-east.
No sooner is the spirit-tide
down and out than on the make again

with the north wind riding her, rock
and knock, slap against the bitten
stanchions abutting the Hard.

Now she's summoning the stars and
they're bursting into her. Light of light.
Still secretive, salty, all-possessing.

YOUR SEA-VOICE

in memoriam Richard Murphy 1927-2018

When I heard you'd died, I'd no idea
we would meet for a second time.
I'd called in fifty years ago
at Derek's bidding (or Michael's?)
en route for Inishmore. All morning
we devoted to monks, penance, islands
and then you jolted me over to Omey
and Saint Fechin's pink granite ruins.
That's where you told me, and wept
as you told me, about the double sorrow.
We sheltered in a sandy hollow
under the first stars, weighed by all
that's fated and inescapable.

You're younger now, you say.
All day I've been scouring this trove
of your early verse for tell-tale signs
– dark histories, nightmares begun.
night drinking dark bog-pools
and drowning is quick and wild graveyards;
the soaked faces of the burnt out men
and their charred Armada wreck
plunges its rusty flukes into my heart,
but there's no more than I expected.

The wind's at worst boisterous,
showers spark, then they're gone,
and what I hear so very clearly
is your persuasive sea-voice,
what I watch is your hand steady
as the boom lifts, and the boat
drops, and above my knees the surge departs, departs...
Yes, much younger, you say, and sailing
to Tir-na-n-Og before nightfall.

THE NORTHERN GODS

for Daisy Jellicoe

Can you hear, dear Daisy,
that rousing horn and the deer-hide drum,
those distant bells on the high pastures?
Can you see that fiddler without a fiddle,
hoicking up his baggy trousers,
singing syllables and beginning to dance?
Listen! That yoik, summoning, capturing
a loved one or a favourite animal, a secret
glade cradled between rock shoulders.

I suspect you think there's very little to be said
for the northern gods, but let me translate them
into their makers, or even into your own
acquaintance. Think of some friend like Bragi
with a gift for poetry; or someone like Frigg
who – excuse my Latin – is a *mater familias*;
some old salt accustomed to iron rations.
A corn-silk blonde? A heavy drinker?
A woman driven by her instincts and passions?

Home from the halls and highlights of Asgard,
I think you'd be smitten by the gods' readiness
to take risks and laugh at themselves,
and admire their unflinching curiosity.
Their rampant sexuality might not be to your liking
but you'd be exhilarated by their energy and wit.
Maybe their childlikeness would disarm you
and you'd mourn at how, gods as they were,
they were fatalists, trapped in time.

Not only this. Look for the lines between lines.
Black scarves swirling, sweeping over tundra,
black grit smoking and scorching boot soles,
black bears, polar bears, packs of wolves,
mountain hares zigzagging across the glaciers
while the midnight sun bounces along the horizon
but then disappears for weeks on end.
Each fire flickers in its own hearth.
Nothing is ever easy on Middle Earth.

Have you ever dreamed you were sitting in the bole
of Yggdrasill, squinting up at the skull
of the white sky, then down into the icy swirl?
Have you heard the vitriol of the dragon,
the corpse-devourer, and seen how the squirrel
whisks it up to the eagle on the topmost branch?
And if, chaste and questing, you too were able
to sip water from the spring, would you
be prepared to make some great sacrifice?

'But the Vikings,' you say, wrinkling your nose,
'weren't they clannish and boastful and suspicious?'
Yes, but these are the defects of virtues.
Remember *Havamal*. 'Never be the first
to strain and break the bonds of friendship...
Never abuse a guest, and be generous
to anyone in need... If you know of some evil,
ensure everyone knows about it... A better man
often comes off worse when swords start talking.'

'What about their violence, then? Their brutality?'
(You persist so prettily). 'What about the blood eagle?'
By all means compare the habits of men and women
a millennium ago with contemporary values
but be very cautious... Can you imagine
what the Vikings would have said about us?
Come now, Daisy. Listen to the words
of a white-haired singer. Allow Idun
 to tempt you with her apples, forever young.

L'ABBAYE-CHÂTEAU DE CAMON

The breath of her. Aliénor is always here
or hereabouts, trailing her wailing
retinue of troubadours.
                                In the love-garden
there's just one orchid, thin as a pencil-lead
(her tress spiralled overnight) with tiny blossoms,
almond-scented,
                        also a single bloom
on the Magnolia Grandiflora – the grandest
in Europe! – luscious and waxen. Before the bride
and her groom departed, there were five,
and one in bud.
                        These, and the bewitching
butterfly-maiden with eyes deep for drowning,
gliding like an acolyte several inches
above the ground.
                        The old leaf showed
his colours only at the last moment
– mottled stone and oaken, dark eye spots.
Then he trembled and faded through a gap
in the crumbling wall.
                                Knowing so very little
about Saint Félicien (without confusing him
with cheese or wild beasts) and not even having
seen his little finger, how can we be so sure
we belong to him, and he to us?
                                        Imagine,
of course. Connect. But falsify nothing.
The suck-and-growl of the pool.
Black holes. Blossoms silently exploding.
The cloister censed by roses.
                                The rondel
of the seasons seems to spin faster, but I see
now there's nothing isolate. Nothing.
All's well beyond words, presently singing.

RICHARD LONG AT HOUGHTON

1 The Magician

Balls of gnats are spinning in the slanting
sunlight, a jet is white-painting
parallel lines, and fourteen people
are standing in a silent circle

watching an old man with a grimy handkerchief
knotted over his head lay slate
after slate in a spiral. He tamps them,
stamps on them (the ground here is uneven),

and it is growing. If they hold their ground
it could whirlpool around them, and they
would become what it is, sweet water
and force. Nothing is impossible.

Clack and clatter! They're listening,
half-dazzled by the shine and sheen,
fourteen apprentices to this wild dream
– this spellbinding, everyday magic.

2 White Waterfall

As when, early, with dew thick on the grass,
a web of gossamer criss-crosses the lawn,
        delicate as lace:

each waterfall here, created but never touched
(mud, energy and space), flows not only to the next
        but home to us.

Begin here perhaps. Is this monster the child
of our own terrors, and our intolerance?
        Is this quiver a ghost?

And is this the head of a dreaming, distant hill
crowned with trees, each branch still articulate
        – oak and beech and ash?

Are these our own arteries, our tendrils
and nerves and cells and ventricles?
        Such finesse!

Each waterfall seethes with sparks and star-splatter,
(accident and gravity). This is how we simplify
        and coalesce.

And laying my words here on these lines,
let me make my marks but lightly,
        and leave with grace.

   3 X Marks the Spot

Crux: unignorable.

Armies of slates, ragged and jagged, not dove.
Pewter. Steel.

Glittering *chevaux de frise*: You could no more
cross it without laceration than cross a field
bristling with barbed wire.

Not Calvary. Not Tau, and not Swastika.
X marks the spot.

Lord of the Four Winds. His lair.

Resting-place for skulls of kings and heroes.

Station. Boundary marker. Fiery not weeping.

Is this nightmare or clean sweep? A dawn
beginning?

Cross your fingers. Everything. Cross your heart.

4 Full Moon Circle

Half this globe is in the dark,
one quarter always advancing
or at war with another.

At my feet the wavelets lap,
they clip and slap each other, and
in the offing they half-open their jaws.

Or is this circle our own field-map
hymned by the sun, the seas of the moon,
each blade and slate ordaining:

'It's late, but still not too late.
Our poor planet. Care for her.
Care for her and she'll care for you.'

JAMES TURRELL'S SKYSCAPE

When the oaks stood aside
we stepped into a glade
where white deer glide
inside their dreams. Beyond
lay the giantesses, shining
and voluptuous, open to caresses.

We came to a wooden tower
and a skyhigh chamber
with benches along the walls,
recliners almost. A leaf drifted in.
Grey wisps unravelling.
Bottomless ocean, upside down.

Houghton Hall

GRAVITY FOR BEGINNERS

Set aside theories and fearsome equations,
likewise galaxies, even saltwater tides.

Gravity is simply mutual attraction.

Words slipping into the mind's casket,
quick rain falling to attending earth.

LIKE THIS

Your dear hands, more especially
your bony wrists, describing how,
at the very last moment
before landing, pink-footed geese
correct their direction, like this,
and divers have to skelter
across water to take off – and how,
at sunrise, ten thousand knots
lifted from the saltmarsh
at Snettisham, and swirled their scarfs,
like this, and then the climbing sun
gilded and blackened them,
and held them to her breast.

SISTERING: DUBAI CREEK

Each old woman bears her shining moon
– one copper, one amber, one nacreous –
and places it gently on the damask.
Their table is well-laid; nothing is wanting.

crescents and quarters at their feet

This is their first night watch. Heads bowed,
the young women sit so still, so close
in their wheel of fears and secrets,
and each clasps her unborn baby.

the breathing water drags and makes

Within their ring of blinking lights,
shoulder to shoulder, thigh to thigh,
the girls plump down on the warm sand.
They cry for the moon, they laugh, and sing.

crescents and quarters at their feet,
the breathing water drags and makes

AS IT IS

for Mary Siemon and Sern Watt

Fitful sunlight. Dry rain, each spark
before it alights evaporating.

Scent of what? Dust, bitterbrush,
wild roses pink-pale,
maybe cow parsnip (*sic*),
needles of fir and Ponderosa:
a composite ancient and sacrosanct,
this ground's memory.

Delete the fanciful.
Tell each component simply as it is.
Grace precedes significance.

Thus: at the top of the dark gully,
one white Alpine butterfly
with a purple gland, three petals
pointed, three frayed...
This scorching paintbrush
rough to my fingertips...

Mare's tails curl high and deep
over Hozemeen and Methow Valley,
the many-tongued river
plunges down from the glacier.

Another dazzle.
A goldfinch starts to dance,
and my own ghost-shadow
stages a comeback.

TUG-OF-WAR

The far bank is frozen and corrugated,
it drops to water stagnant, winter-curdled,
jammed with sodden leaves, delicate bones
and Oasis cans; the near bank is springloaded
with sharp-eared aconites and snowdrops.
There's shrill whistling in the brakes
and screaming in the air, white wings tacking,
making heavy weather of it.

Stumbling along the bilious hedgerows
half-strangled with glistening ivy,
one fellow is wearing a feathered hat
and one shouldering his accordion...
Most have seen it before, and they all
know the way of it, this war
across the common stream.
Three o'clock. The third Sunday in February.

Advancing along either bank, everyone
comes face to face below the crumbling
horsebridge where Bucks and Oxon meet
– the place where as children they played
poohsticks and swore blood secrets –
as many as either village can muster,
but well down on last year's numbers.
The great grey trunks soar over them.

Scuffing beech mast, staring into sky-pools
above and below them, each side unties
the rope hitched to a branch. There's room
for everyone, laughing and jostling.
Nothing stretches as long as time
before beginning, but at last the front men
fall silent. They dig in their heels
as if the seasons of their lives depend on it.

At first the two teams give not an inch.
They lurch, they grunt, and their coaches
synchronise each haul, each stay.
Perched on the steep shoulders
of the bridge their supporters howl.
But now, on the far bank, the first man
slithers down the mud-slide on his butt
and his whole line has to give ground.

What happens? How do they recover,
and then regain much more than they lost?
Muscle, sheer bloody-mindedness.
Their new coach? A new dispensation?
On the near bank, the leader slips
through snowdrops, the second staggers
over him, and half the team are dragged,
shouting and swearing, into the stream.

Commotion. Confusion. But after
the flurry, all the stabilising rituals
hold – the contestants climb up and crowd
on to the bridge, pink and sweating;
and, as usual, the accordion's time has come.
Wind-shear. Roaring beeches. Needles of rain.
They shout and laugh, and raise glasses
of damson wine to the absent sun.

Suspicion, though, feeds on itself,
and many folks reckon it's all a fix.
Why, the outcome's been the same
for as long as anyone can remember.
Some people are blaming the fearsome winter,
some climate change, most just don't know.
There's to be a joint parish meeting but, even so,
how can things ever be natural again?

MY MOTHER'S INKPOT

When I severed the top joint of my left thumb
I opened the floodgates. My children's children
shrieked, and for much of that afternoon I built
churches with steeples, and conjured shining coins
out of air, and retaught my rheumatic fingers
to fashion snapping shadow-monsters.
Mah-zheek! they cried. *Mah-zheek! More!*

When my father performed much the same sleights,
my mother often sat at her marquetry desk
and dashed off letter after letter, all wit
and fervour. She regarded a wide margin
or an untouched inch in the way
a gardener might view an unsown drill
or border – an opportunity wasted.

Over and again she drained the deep well dry
but never once was I magicked by that,
not until the morning after she'd invited me
to refill it – silver, quietly gleaming.
I saw how the heavy lid had lifted;
this posy of primulas, lemon and orange,
were springing and spilling out of it.

HERE, ON THE HEADLAND

Here, on the headland
lifted last week
and still unploughed,
I scooped up dusty seedlings
that had slipped through the grader
– sufficient for a meal or two –
and stuffed my pockets.

Then in the topmost corner
where tattered hedgerows meet
I found little heaps
almost the size of molehills
raised but dropped
when the turning harvester
sloughed them off.

Incomparable, I thought,
for any observer:
here in the wings, half-curtained,
yet still in light of light
with a sightline right down
to the foreshore and the anchorage
– pale eucharists at my feet.

EN ROUTE

Isn't there always some unscheduled halt
with its attendant wonders? Now and then
the marvellous or the monstrous
but more often the humdrum
– a reclamation yard, or the smell
of an autumn bonfire; this siding, say,
choked with dusty purple nettles,
an ochre butterfly flickering over them.

Even the weathered inspector
is half-surprised, half-smiling
at your single, steadfast gaze.
Whatever is. Maybe early, very likely
late, you know this is the one true line
and now you're well en route.

ALBANO

Soon after Albano hoicked his sheep into the bath of his three-bedroom house in Cherry Hinton and cut its throat, we parted company.

My verse, *Nomads*. That's how we met. I recall not a single line, but he was taken with the rough-and-toughness and terseness of it.

And that's how he saw himself. Stocky. Battling. Stamping out his staging-posts.

A Resistance leader.

Champion of causes. Hitch-hiking. Karagiosis. Mandatory Mandarin in all secondary schools.

Half-bald, head like a cannon-ball.

His poem for his mother made me squirm. My eyeballs burned. Our shared room was too small.

Architect of churches too roseate for the Home Counties: of his deceased Italian father, he spoke very little.

So very generous. Above all, the way he threshed my poems and blitzed my translations.

So scornful. On the back of an envelope he mapped my progression: *Faber Poetry Editor. Poet Laureate. Knighthood.* (Well, no, none of those!) 'Is that really all you want?'

The last letter I had from him was after his Pinochet protest and release from the football stadium in Santiago.

Did we not have a single friend in common?

His birthday gift: a precious edition of *Cuchulain of Muirthemne*, inscribed 'For Kevin, to stop him selling this'.

Each gave and took what he needed. So what was I to him? Younger brother, acolyte, itching post. Still so unquestioning and so hidebound, not quite unredeemable.

Moth memories? No. Grappling-hooks.

When his browbeaten wife wrote years later, I was unable to answer,
unable to throw her words away.

BEECHES

Never a green boy – a student, say,
of coppicing and bud-burst, never a disciple
of the nomad bodgers, propped half the day
against a bavin – but the way he fingertipped
to the fork in his climbing-tree, high above
all the initials and graffiti, and reached
upwards as beeches do...
                              Aged nine,
he staged a protest beneath the doomed
trees at Ladymede, and cried when he heard
the terrible grinding. Their toppling haunted
him, and for years he dreamed that beech trees
were growing into him.
                              How each leaf
looks like its selfsame tree, and the way
its roots brace; kinship, intelligence,
spelter and the principles of turning,
– yes, of course he was eager to find out
all these things, but later.
                              Mid-April.
It's very mild, almost still, one by one at last
the leaves are falling. Each twists, though,
or spurts forward, or slides in mid-tango,
loops, maybe rises again. As he lunges
after them, the old man laughs, stumbles
and begins to name them.
                              Copper and Rust,
Shy, Sideways, Surge, Lonesome, Only,
Wounded, Wonder, Wanderer, Tawny Gold,
Trickster, Memory.

THE NEW FAMILIAR

It's always the same, and never.
Under our feet the ground starts
to heave, the skyline becomes toothy,
and soon there'll be that first sight
of snow, is it, all of fifty miles off,
unless it's only limestone.

Our host conducts us up wide steps
scalloped by centuries of hooves
and halfway along the cloister corridor,
then swings open *Les Coquelicots*.
Trumpet sunlight. Welcoming shadows.
Leaving leisurely, he says, there's to be
a trip tomorrow morning to hunt
for wild orchids, 'and a great surprise
this year'. Would we care to come?

We've crossed half this continent again
and arrive at this: what we crave
is no longer the unbelievable,
the idyllic or hitherto inaccessible
– not the old imperatives beyond
the horizon, but the new familiar.

THROUGH A GLASS, DARKLY

Tumbleweed somersaults, it bundles right
along the dreadful rim. But in a stone hide
we stumbled on an old brass reflectoscope
– black onyx, darkened glass – and saved
ourselves from the worst of our atrocities.

Unless you're a demon or some temptress
why on Earth would you look down not up?
Peering through fingers into appalling depths
(five thousand million years of gneiss and schist)
desolate, flooded, cancerous, burning.

Far better to look up. Raise your eyes
to cloud-castles, light on the mountains,
silver ghost-paths of dream and intention.
Unlimited by flesh or bone, the gods
have never lived in ditches or craters.

Yet even so, with our tarred soles and muddy
hands, there'll be no blinding revelation.
We can only watch for what we may
not see or, if we do, just glimpse
through soothing shades, and bear witness.

RECONCILIATION

I'm no flat earthist, but don't dispute
the world's four corners have been held up
by dwarfs, which has nothing whatsoever
to do with the Four Corners monument,
which has nothing to do with the
petrified gods of the Navajo and Vikings.

How entrancing the mind is,
crossing so hungrily between planes,
wrestling with the complex and knowing
when to suspend disbelief, and how
to reconcile opposites, accepting
that answers always beg questions.

And yet to sit for an hour or so
beside this turbulent salt creek
and watch a cloud of dark knots
flying as one, or hear the single yap
of rigging responding to what I cannot
even see: this is homecoming.

It's true, nothing is irreconcilable
but, far from unhopeful, the old mind
begins to tire, no longer as restless
as this tide on the make, always
insistent (despite the dams
and groynes) on its links and passages.

In the blue hour, a single prayer suffices.

SHOULDER ON

Even if there's any reason why this
has happened, there's no need to reason why.
Better to regard it as a kind of blessing
like a next-to-neap tide stealthily
replenishing the drained, muddy creek,
or the last red-gold on a far field.

Isn't it an invitation to engage
while you can, aware each word
and silence entail responsibilities?
Accept interruptions. Shoulder on.
Try again to say something worth saying
without knowing yet quite what it is.

SILENT ORDER

Words again. Words.
How am I to put them
in service to silence?

The stretch-fields here
are so rich with promises,
memories, never endings.

Silver-green with flint arrowheads,
golden with proud
and finicky bones,

Or look at the rage,
the flags and rags of oaks
only last year stricken,

the daily drumroll of clouds
towering and threatening,
gentling into dusk showers.

Let me absorb all this
and begin again. Let me commit
to the slow work of unsaying.

True, what I've tried to say
– there's no gainsaying it,
but this unravelling, this denying

myself years of stitchwork,
and all I never questioned
I was born to do…

No longer to sing, to share,
obedient only
to this one calling.

LA PLAINE DE LA MADELEINE

Well above the hamlet on its tipsy ledge
there was a meadow. One path scrambled up to it.
It was passionate with wildflowers and unvisited,
innocent of whatever was happening below.
On hands and knees I crawled along the side
where you could drop off the edge of the world.

Long ago, waking hot and hectic
or shocked by some dream, I used to splash
my face with water biting as a mountain stream,
lie back and climb that rocky path again.
Turbanned lily, gentian, orange poppy,
soldanella… names I no longer remember.

Each breathing midnight now, unsure I'll return,
I realise I'm doing the same. I'll do the same.

IN A NORFOLK GARDEN

An Idyll for Peter Scupham and Margaret Steward

Little clusters of guests are sitting
beneath the tortured oaks, a few on tartan rugs,
most on the jaundiced grass,
and others are lined up on recliners
like survivors from some TB sanatorium
soaking in this late August sunlight.
Something's going on in front of them:
a pair of ancients, gesticulating.
Their backs are turned but I can hear
their words, even at this distance.
    Jesu, Jesu, the mad days that I have spent!
    And to see how many of my old acquaintance
    are dead... We shall all follow, cousin...
Got it! It's those two country justices.
    Certain, 'tis certain; very sure, very sure.

*

While I'm still listening to these two truth-tellers,
hollow-eyed and glum, playing at playmaking,
a wizened monk, maybe a Carthusian
or some Carmelite home from the Holy Land,
grabs my collar.
    'Norfolk!' he croaks,
'Norfolk! Satan on the road to Hell
ruined Norfolk as he fell.' His breath
smells of honey. I readjust my sprig
of sea-lavender, and politely refer him
to Sir John who's on his way
with his old flame, Billa,
and expected around teatime.

*

Over there, that's George Barker,
black drill-eyed, well oiled already
and the sun's not yet at the zenith.
He's hectoring the pinstripe murderer
who awarded me a bar to my DFC,

then finished me off at Biggin Hill,
presently strangling a very pretty
young whitebeam with his spider fingers.
Why are they pincering poor George Szirtes?
What's going on? Is this some nomen league,
celebrants of a tribune martyred
in Nicomedia, venerated only
in England, Portugal and Albania?

*

Surrounded by cats and herbs, mossy statues
and stagnant little pools fringed with white lace,
what grows in this sacred space
are words, well-watered, thinned
and pleached and flowering – year upon year
of readings and recitations grave and gay
by lights very bright and distinctly limited,
generations of poets, some with their families,
attending to their roots and calling.

*

You'd heard that several guests had died,
some long since, and that's the case,
but it's scarcely surprising to be surrounded
by like minds and 'affable presences'.
Almost everyone's present at this assembly
they wouldn't miss for anything.
Look! There's Skelton, our first laureate, rapping
with a young man who spent all morning
choosing which cravat to wear
(mauve, yes, mauve, I think so), and then how to tie it.
But who's that with bells on his ankles,
hopping and skipping between the weedy beds
and warbling in his annoying falsetto:
>   *A Country Lasse browne as a berry...*
>   *something, something... heart as merry,*
>   *Cheekes well fed and sides well larded*
>   *Every bone with fat flesh guarded...*
Got it again! It's Will Kemp,
darling of the groundlings

and dancer all the way from London to Norwich,
his eyes always sharp for the next chance,
a 'Marrian in his Morrice daunce'.

*

As for Old Hall, and its 'long marriage
of queen strut, king post', its mysteries
'exposed by sweat, patched together with lime,
stage-paint, a little imagination',
let it rest today on its laurels.
Our paths lead out from it,
all our words come home to it
and its 'gatekeepers and custodians'.
Everyone here knows that.
> *Love it. Choose it. Whatever the words mean*
> *Hauled from the moil, the tumult in the head*
> *And heart.*

*

Our host rises, gleaming and genial,
bent double almost. First he rehearses a few
regrets and no-shows, among them Frances Cornford,
Lilias Rider Haggard and dear Wystan,
then announces a couple of surprise arrivals:
two more Georges, on horseback,
both from silly Suffolk. Very strange.
> *When tides were neap, and, in the sultry day*
> *Through the tall bounding mud-banks made their way,*
> *Which on each side rose swelling, and below*
> *The dark warm flood rose silently and slow...*

Ah, Crabbe! George Crabbe, my words, hard-won,
echo your own. My creeks and staithes of Brothercross,
their small gains shored against struggle and loss...

*

The quick and the dead,
home-grown and foreigner,
seventeen poets now stand and deliver.
Several of them are audible.
Sail and Brownjohn, Mole and Griffiths and Underwood
and last, as befits our senior poet:

Speaking as best I may, or as I might.
If the day failed and all there was was night,
I look for something which could still be light.
Yes, that's Anthony Thwaite.
It's very nearly too late.

*

'Where's William Cowper?' I ask my host.
'My namesake on my mother's side.
'A sage beneath a spreading oak.'

He gives me a melancholy look. 'Is that so?
'I don't rightly know. Neither does he.'

*

This blistering heat. These tumblers of red wine.
Butterfly flicker... Dear creatures, marinade those hours.
Where, pray, in this whole kingdom
is there any living ancient place,
any garden trained, still wild, a dream
of an assembly in the least like this?

Old Hall Poetry Picnic, South Burlingham

Harald in Byzantium (2022)

1

When I was a boy, I was a boy.
I wrestled with my elder brothers
and made myself sick on gluts of blueberries
we picked. I flew kites.

It was those blades at Stiklestad
cut my childhood out of me.

There's a poem about how fate can finish off
anyone, even an unfated man,
if his bravery is wanting.
His bravery, but also his discipline.
If one man breaks the shield-rampart
all his companions suffer.

Each of us could do with a magic reindeer coat
purchased at some extortionate price
but life's not like that, there's no easy way out.

My men here understand this.
They know the watchwords:
forethought, caution, action, effect.
I'll brook no disobedience. None at all.

2

At Stiklestad I was fifteen
and still too eager. An older man
saved me from myself

when that Swede's spear
opened my entrails. Then his family
hid me all winter, and they fed me.

Promises come cheap; honouring them seldom.
But he kept his word. At my bidding
he sailed south, and fought with me in Sicily.

Each of us needs around us not only
young men but those who knew us young.
Home in Trondheim, I'll seek him out again.

3

Garthar, Garthar, not here,
not there, but in between.

In her forests she will grant you
nothing but nettles, thorns, teeth,
night eyes shining. There's no escape.

Her hair, wild black, a dozen times
she winds it around you...

*

But at Bosphorus, they welcomed my dragon-prow,
waving from their swarm of dugouts
or cobles or knars or whatever they call them.

Sails blue as promises, pink as flamingos
and green and bitter as kelp.

I was not born yesterday.
Sweet today is often sour tomorrow.

4

My fjord winds to a turf-roof
and the glacier's blue teeth.
I can hear the quernstone
grinding the salt in the northern sea.

Your smooth-skinned channel slides
between bluffs. Even when the water
is pink, violet, you can see her depths,

her rounded white rocks shimmering.
I do not know where you are taking me
but I have no choice, only an imperative.

5

for Aygün Catak

The eyes of my women
are dawn-grey, dawn-blue.
Here, they are black stars,

and a little painted fingernail
achieves more than a northern
screech or pitchfork.

In a climate cold and wet
there's very little blaze,
not even much smoulder.

I have resolved to stay
in Miklagard a little longer.

6

Three Anglians have arrived at court.
Thorold understands their muddy tongue
and says they come from Jorvik.

They tell him they're pilgrims
suffering for love of the White Christ,
journeying they care not where.
Oh?

To have travelled so far
not as traders, missionaries or messengers
means only they had much to get away from:
not just some debt or a furious woman;
their own death-shadows, no doubt.

They've told Thorold they're ready
to serve the Empress –
but in this benighted place
a dozen counsellors are arguing
about whether to trust and enlist them,
and if not, whether...

Either they'll be sent packing
or I'll be detailed
to take care of them
like those Burgundians.

One of them reminds me of Guttorm,
my half-brother.

7

This week another boatload of young bucks sailed in,
their mouth stuffed with oaths,
and, as usual, they know all the answers.

This tide of refugees, for instance
– more, many more than shoals of herring in the fjord.

It's better to go for the jugular, is it,
better to stem the tide at source?
Yes, commit all us Varangians to an invasion.
No, better to meet them at the crossing-places
and cut off their right hands
and send them home.

Well then, extend our borders...
As if this Empire's not already bulbous and porous.
And who would govern the governors?

Ah! Here's a thinker.
Better long words than actions, he advocates.
Better persuasion then incursion.
Have these refugees grasp that our welcome
will be strictly conditional – they'll be un-citizens
– arse-lickers, and slaves.

And this one is a bloody missionary... Ye gods!
Do you really believe that if we baptise them
they'll troop back to Jerusalem?
Have you the least idea what they're fleeing from?
Have you never heard of the power of dreams?

I've served here for nine half-years.
There cannot be a single strategy,
there can be no checkmate.
The next right choice
is all we can play for.

    ♟

I've been told
half-a-dozen of my men
have been bad-mouthing me
since we set foot in Sicily.

That one,
and the one from Kiev over there...
I know their names.

Pretending they mean to murder me
tonight in my own tent,
my faithful two body-men
will approach them
to enlist their support,

and if any of them agree
I'll have them hanged in the morning.
Breakfast for buzzards.

After that, I'll call for new oaths.
I serve the Empress,
and each Varangian here serves me.

9

'Chickens! Harald, don't waste your time on them.
And that includes your elder brothers.'

I was three when I pulled the king's beard
and he laughed, but his pupils were black pinpricks.

No one can accuse that fucking Turk
of being quick-witted, let alone witty,
and the way he squawks at me
curdles my cheeks. But he's wily and stubborn,
and in the name of our common cause, Holy Empire,
I'll do well to study his tactics
and how to proceed against him.

10

Trapped in the mixing-bowl of some hill troll.
Scorching wind from Africa... red dust whirling
round me, red dust in my throat, my gut.
Then a raven flops down and one-eyes me.

'Red dust? No, not only. Harald, you are blood.
You are memory. That stained field...
Wherever you are, whoever your enemy,
when you raise your right arm, strike for me.'

11

Grasses soon grow on a little-trodden road
but leader and led can never rub shoulders.
That's the cost. Have it said
Harald always understood that of all gifts
friendship freely-given is the greatest.

*

No blood-friend tells you
only what you want to hear.

You can add that truth to Havamal.
And here's another:

Self-love is sponge.
Self-respect is forged.

12

Slingstones have their limitations.
With my battering-ram I'll breach
their soaring walls. And I will dispose
of Gyrgir, that Armenian lout…
I will do this, I will do that,
and that and that. But who can say
whether you will lie with me again,
shining in your cocoon of Jewish silks?

13

The delicate contraption of your right ankle,
the downy crooks of your arms,
your swan-neck.

They give me back
my elbows and knees, the plates
of my shoulder-bones, the thud,
thud of my heart.

Dear Gods,
I who will rule
the whole northern world…
My head is thumping. My heart spinning.

14

I become breathless. I am tormented.
I would trade days
to feel again on my palms
the weight of your perfect breasts,
to hear once more the way
you sweet-mouthed my name.

15

Let the gods grow old.
Let them become mumbling imbeciles.
Let them become incontinent.

Grant me one night
in your apple-garden
forever young,

and I will outgod the gods.

16

Many times I've slept under this rough canvas
– my men hawking and swearing all around me – and often
enough I've choked on stinking scat,
listened to hooting owls and slept beneath stars,
all too often wrapped in my own arms.

A spice-trader from Split asked me last week:
'Where you come from? Where you going?'
Each question invites the next: 'What is home?'

17

Rót... skát... traust...
I like the t... t of the Icelanders,
Distinct, and light as a bleb.
Charming as a scamp's tip-tilted nose.
t... t... still hanging in mid-air
after its word has disappeared.

18

Our rosy-cheeked Empress, Princess of Peace...
          Purple-pouched, more like.
Silence! Who said that?
          Ghastly hag. Old tombstone.
          Murderous Pumpkin.
Shut your traps or I'll slice
your tongues, I'll tattoo your testicles.
Some men close to our Empress,
our Princess of Peace, have put it about
she's scoffing at me, and says
I'm nothing but the young son of some troll.

You are, Harald! Harald, you are!
That harridan, she's jealous.
She's purple and fifty-four!
Silence!

19

Mermaids?
A mixed blessing! I've met several.

That moon-mermaid in Syria
on my way back from Jerusalem:
every man and woman worshipped her
although she was made of marble.

As a young boy
I was overwintering in Unst
– a miserable settlement if ever there was –
when a fisherman was trapped by a mermaid's song.
She tried to drown him
but his companions stoned her, and drove her off.

One of my men asserts
a good many of the Irish are descended
from mermaids.

When I'm king I'll tether one
in a pool brimming with saltwater
– also a siren.
They can sing together.

Wise men will teach them our tongue
and ask them all they know
about healing and snaring and underwater,
and what stories they've heard
concerning Aegir and Ran.

20

I woke from a dream
of my mother's first home on the fiord.

The men greeted me, but not as one of their own.
A stranger was perching in that seat
Thorgeir forged for my mother
from iron bars and little strips.
Then I saw him at the far end of the staithe.
I'd know his wading walk anywhere,
but he was less certain. Knees buckling.

I can go no further. Not one step.
First I have to come back.
That's what I told him.
'You understand that?'

No morning for leaning
into the wind, shadow ribs swept through us.
The water was uneasy, and the islet winked.

'The old are often wise,' he said.
'They may hang with the hides
and flap with the pelts
and rock with the guts in the wind,
but shrivelled skins often give wise advice.
Aegir will smooth your sea-path,' he told me.
'Allfather will fate you to come home.'

'Thorgeir? Deaf as a door-stopper
for the last seven years.'
So said the men.

21

Halfway up, my guide paused
beside a glittering stream and his little daughter
waded in and picked up white pebbles.
This source, he said me in his laughable Norse,
gallops north. He opened his pale palms.
Novgorod. Ladoga. Baltic.

Unaware of his insolence, he reached up
and tried to put an arm around my shoulders.
I shook it off.

Over there, he said, pointing to a ridge
no more than a shout away,
that source south. Black Sea. Miklagard.

Time was, I didn't hesitate,
not for one moment.
So eager, so full-blooded.
Was my heart that wild?
That unbridled?

Time is, I've got my eye on Time
and what survives it: followers,
the golden crown, hard-edged fame.

Tomorrow, I'll make my peace with Jaroslav
and ask again for the hand of his bracelet-goddess.
I'll point my black prow north.

22

The old scalds shared what they knew
but it isn't true, not half of it

though half my men swallow it.
They've crossed deep waters
and still think like children.

We see only shadows of the gods,
and they've very little interest in us.
What they're said to have said
is only what we wish they'd say.

But there's one…
In my dreams I often see you
standing in the shade.

Not Frigg, giver of flax, not Fulla,
not even one of the holy thirteen.

But I have always known you,
and now I need you.
Tell me your true name.

23

I am become like a bottle in the smoke.
If I can trust my translator,
that's what one psalmist sings.
But what's the point of unmanning ourselves,
and declaring our weaknesses?
Many a lad has lived too long
under his father's thumb, and many
haven't mastered how to hoist a sail.
Because of some fool, good plans
have been misunderstood or else stillborn…
No! give me a lump of gammelost
with the tang of mouldering Vikings,
give me fire from a bottle to wash it down.
I'll be true to those who follow me
in the names of firebrands before me.
Let me be blood and flames.

New Poems (unpublished)

THE GHOST BECK

Where she rises when she chooses
to break cover is some way below
Chalk Hill Wood though not down as far
as Barrow Pit Meadow but exactly where
her source is the dowser cannot tell

saying she surfaces each seventh year
is no more than an old wives' tale
come each spring the pond beside
the surgery turbanned with old bulrushes
starts swelling filling and deciding
as often as not to overflow
and making haste for the Hoste
coursing through the Green
flashing or glimmering surprising
drivers on their last leg to the coast
and splashing the windscreens
of those who disrespect her

until tiring no longer diaphanous
faltering fading she becomes
little more than a dark stain and then
one late afternoon just disappearing
a ghost lost to herself again

THE BALLAD OF MR HERRING

Mr Herring was having dark dreams
about his dappled lane,
the one that climbs halfway to heaven
then drops to sea-level again.

When he retired he bought half an acre
– his life savings all in one go.
He dug it and he levelled it
and raised a bungalow

for himself and his wife Cynara,
up at the top with a sea-view.
Friends admired their sparing lives
and the way they made do,

all the neat rows of veg and flowers.
Pickles, chutneys and jams,
and pot-pourri and lavender bags:
the Herrings were happy as clams.

Old Herring was a decent man
– you could say a 'good ole bor'.
He gave to several charities
and had fought in the First World War.

Some cleverclogs remarked how he
was set fair from week to week,
while his gentle wife was cool,
sweet air on the cheek.

So it's scarcely surprising
that ordinary folk,
people like the Herrings, partial
to a shandy and a quiet smoke,

followed their example, and built
little cottages in the speckled lane;
some were flint, some were chalk,
no two were quite the same.

Well, old Mr Herring wasn't long gone
when his home was tabbed by a scout.
Then something awful happened.
A bigwig from London bought Cynara out.

He didn't give a fig about the cost,
he just *adored* the place.
But did that bastard ever meet
Cynara face to face?

The first thing he did was flatten it.
'This shack! Our second home?
Without a master suite, a games room,
cinema… gymnasium!

A hungry tribe soon descended
– investors, lawyers, bankers.
And some called locals who wouldn't sell
swedes and effing wankers.

They erected castles on tiny plots
– neo-Gothic piles for multi-millionaires.
Monstrosities, unoccupied
for most months of the year.

It was all more than poor Herring could bear:
their darkling dreams, his suffering lane.
He prised open the lid of his pine coffin,
stood up and screamed. He screamed in pain.

LOVE ENTIRE

I scanned the contents page
then turned to *Love Entire*.

No more than a pencilled line
or two. She was not there

but elsewhere, unknown,
and patient always.

What did Plato say?
Once human nature was entire,

and the name for our desire,
our pursuit of that is love.

Again I faced the white page,
and now I wrote to vow it.

ATTEMPT

When, like a young gymnast, you vaulted
the five-barred gate then seriously offered me
a sweet cigarette, I laughed and asked you
whom the alm belonged to – little more, really,
than a sweet mound stitched with wildflowers
at the foot of the colossal mountains –

and you allowed it was your own, yours
and your family's, then dropped to your hands
and knees, and tousled your cropped hair.
'Halfway here,' you told me, 'between those glaciers
and the Rhône, rushing. Orchids unknown,
monsieur, are they what you're searching for?'

No, not those. Not this easiness
and earthly beauty, lambent. I waved my stick
towards the massive silence. 'I'm nearly there
and must try to hear it. Whatever's been,
and what's to come. While I still can,
let me attempt to quarry it.'

A BEECH BOWL

for Lynda on her sixtieth birthday

Where you've so often stood
and understood
above the spread white wings
high on the hill

a beech tree fell
beside an age-old knoll

In friendship a man shouldered
and carried to a kind of god
an almighty branch

and as he turned and leavened it
the years and wounds
grown into it
grew only more beautiful

Given to me now given to you
this gift from the tree herself
and her green sisters

this lop-sided circle
of birdsong and underlight
of root and reach

of love itself
unending and incarnate

HIS CARE, THE HESITATIONS

It wasn't his words
but when their attempts and alternatives
faltered
To try even to echo them
falls far short
again words want

And then there was no need for them
because what he'd been speaking of
spoke itself

I can only write
we were all one body
in the burning light
so fierce so steady
the hot tears
finding their likeness in each of us

and of how we knew
it was not the saying
but his care
the hesitations
dear life springing from them

SHRUTI-VENO

Not just Indrani
          at whose silvered
ankles I sat for all of two hours,
but a sly storyteller too
who guided us between worlds.
That first evening was incomparable.

On the second we welcomed
a well-oiled wise man,
naked to the navel. I marvelled
at the way he answered many
of my questions before I asked them.

Then through the London smog
my father struggled home
lugging a shruti-veno.
I pumped the bellows
and brought it to life.

Drone and fiddle,
fiddle and drone,
each reaching for the other.
Now after sixty years
I understand the truth of them:

what's past, its matter, its weight
to fathom as best I can;
a dancer at midnight
still first-footing it, pitching
all that's happening.

AN ALMS-BASKET

in celebration of the 75th anniversary of the Almshouse Association

Who was it said
The past is never dead. It's not even past.
We know the truth of this.
Let me tell you a story.

One woman, one man,
this is how things begin.
For those without to shelter within
you've opened your arms for a millennium.

Often, when we enter,
there's something in the air
common to hallowed ground
– a church or cloister, a secret garden.

A freight of memories,
a flight at one remove
from circling atrocities, a place where we sense
more nearly what we can be.

Care is so hardy.
You lop branches, you modify,
and your guardian trees multiply.
In each constituency they thrive.

Here the humdrum
and prodigious walk hand in hand.
Community and dream
– their common stream the human heart.

There's no reason to labour this.
A decent provision for the poor
is the true test of civilisation.
The words of Dr. Johnson.

An old boy accosted me.
Your almshouses! What are they then
when they're at home?
Not pubs? Not safehouses?

I did my best to explain.
'Some ancient, some modern,
They're local, affordable, a charity.
For those in need – and our own.'

Ah! Got it. Go on, then!
Onward, yes. Today and tomorrow…
Dear friends, this is the story.
You are the story.

HOLDERNESS: SPURN HEAD

Not easily won, this spur of England
where the twists, jinks and dog-legs go on
and on. The barley has broken the red
again, it's sharpening its spears
beneath the vast sky-acres
bright for an hour, but then sagging,
massing only to disperse.

You couldn't call them merry
but rank upon rank,
and each rank a different hue,
the army on the long beach
have locked shoulders.
They jig and clatter.

How well used they are to defiance
and attrition. Any lasting change
will have to be enforced on them.
And all this before the underbelly,
– stinking pill-boxes,
poisonous foxgloves all the way
to Skeffling and far beyond.

THE ACCIDENT OF POETRY

Still half-thinking about Kazakhstan,
while inspecting our orchard and little veg. garden,
its multi-coloured apple forests,
I saw a muntjac had cropped the cot-splits,
but at least the ragged fence
had stopped him from getting
at the nine young iris again,
now showing some form in their hospital bed.

So it goes,
like de la Mare's fly, and Rossini's splodge.
First the intention, and the hesitant steps
often going nowhere.
But then the accident of poetry.

I pottered along the green nave
towards my waymarker, certain
I'd risk a bite of the black apple
if only I could find one.

MOTH-LIGHT: 1959

for Angela (neé Platten)

So you too remember those moths.
How wildly they flapped and jammed,
and crowded in on that furious light.

At Griff House I was allowed
that little room where Mary Ann
daydreamed and began to write.

I coached my pupil each morning
on home ground: Latin, French, English.
Afternoons were more complicated.

But on the last, come teatime, your mother
drove you over from Meriden,
and we played scrappy tennis.

It was much too hot, and you
ballooned balls into the nettles.
Even trudging back for those

snared in the netting made us tetchy,
and your hemstitched white skirt
was smeared red, and gritty.

After dark, we watched them: cinnabar
and scalloped oak, brimstone, mint,
hawk-moth. So murderous, so innocent.

Tightly, then tender, we held hands
– your right, my left – and I remember
thinking we were so nearly lovers.

TUULI

We danced at midnight on the sopping deck.
Each time the rusty ferry rocked
we all piled up against the railings.

Only as we nosed between those skerries
and the islands of revenants did you
tell me. You rounded your pale pink lips.

More breath and sound than substance,
you blew on my left cheek, and then
disembarked at Marienhamn.

I called, I tried to wave away the dark,
and even now, long since in dock, reaching
for the north-east wind, I lurch.

EACH

Down by the pond and early, every
became each.
                    Wizards in silver bumper cars
could never match the skills of those seven
whirligigs. Squatting by the reach
of stones our birds bathe from,
I spotted a rare Norfolk hawker,
watched an azure chaser hitch
himself to his mate. One chaffinch
and a bully blackbird, two vagrant
oystercatchers... Our grizzled hare lolloped
towards me, the first lily showed me
the tips of her pink wings...
Each blue-green blade of each iris,
each whisk and whistle, quiver, stitch:
I want so very little more than this.

MISSING PERSON

The way she could rise a little above
herself, and float across a room…
On their knees, her witnesses vowed
it was a gift from God, but others
said it was witchy, unnatural.
She was known for her disturbing
paintings of the coupled Marys.
She went by several names and
referred to herself as a novice.

Up at the ruined château
for half-term (camping, barbeques,
and risking the dangerous shit-hole)
lads from Puylaurens and round about
joked that one day they'd spot her
rising, on her way to heaven.
Then at Hunter's Moon, the same boy
who saw Eden through an arrow-slit
swore he did just that.

Thing is, that was the same night
the floating girl disappeared.
No one knows how, or where
she was going. She had repainted
the little room she rented
(17 Rue d'Etoile) eau de nil.
It was suffused with perfume:
lily of the valley. All information,
please, to la Mairie, Lavelanet.

LA PART DES ANGES

No matter and no mist,
not a speck, mote or crystal.
Below her tapering neck, her apron
is lettered with muted gold, gris
and siskin, watermarked with twists,
twirls, buds and curlicues we see
when they catch the light.

Fragrant spirit, oaken,
breathless angels are said to sip
before their migration – a bright-eyed
congregation we see, or might,
only at oyster light, poised
to unweigh, and upon
a point, spiralling upwards.

> *Domaine de la Noblaie*
> *Chinon*

BEFORE WORDS FAIL

> *To every thing there is a season,*
> *and a time to every purpose under the heaven:*
>   ECCLESIASTES 3:1

Before shoulders sag and stick-legs buckle,
before teeth rattle and eyes grow misty

Before heights become fearsome and
journeys troublesome

When sudden birdsong is alarming, and
sweet daughters sing out of tune

When even honey bees are irksome though
the apple is in blossom

A time to be born, and a time to die;
  a time to plant, and a time to pluck up
  that which is planted;
A time to kill, and a time to heal;
  a time to break down, and a time to build up;

Before desire slackens

Before the alphabet scrambles, before
words fail:

A time to weep, and a time to laugh;
  a time to mourn, and a time to dance;
a time to cast away stones, and a time to gather
  stones together; a time to embrace,
  and a time to refrain from embracing;

The wind drives south, the wind
wafts north...
One generation stumbles, the next skips
and dances in...
There is nothing new under the sun

A time to get, and a time to lose; a time to keep,
  and a time to cast away;
A time to rend, and a time to sew; a time to keep
  silence, and a time to speak;

Before deadly clouds mass and close ranks
Before grids seize and turbines fall silent,
before the sea curdles

Before plates grind and widen and this poor
planet spins

A time to love, and a time to hate; a time of war,
  and a time of peace.

Before the hub blackens and explodes,
before the moon wastes and constellations
are snuffed out

Before dust falls to dust and the spirit soars:
with a handful of quietness draw near to
your creator.

NOTES

p. 33 'Glum's Warping': the rudiments of this poem derive from a story collected by Jon Arnason in *The Folktales and Fairy Tales of Iceland*.

p. 49 'Postcards from Kodai': Kodaikanal is a hill station in the Western Ghats. More than seven thousand feet high, it was developed as a retreat by the English who frequented it during the summer months when life became unbearably hot on the plains.

p. 77 'The Painting-Room': poems 1, 3, 5, 7 and 9 take details from John Constable's (1776-1837) drawings and paintings as their starting points.

p. 129 'Pearls and Diamonds': a diamond-and-pearl tiara belonging to Queen Sonja of Norway was stolen from Garrards, the London jewellers (where it had been sent to be cleaned) during an armed robbery on 5 February 1995.

p. 139 'Translation Workshop: Grit and Blood': the first two lines come from 'The Battle of Maldon' (lines 312-13). The second stanza translates them and the remainder of Byrhtwold's exhortation.

p. 148 'Footsore: In Seach of Chinese Cellist': Burwood is a suburb of Sydney in Australia. After hearing the cellist and her peers (all nationally known as soloists, in Australia to learn English) play for pennies on Circular Quay, I went to Burwood, hoping to hear them for a second time.

p. 155 'Notes on a Field-Map': based on an 1842 tithe map of Walsham-le-Willows.

p. 156 'Anasazi Woman': the Anasazi were the precursors of the present-day Pueblo Indians of New Mexico and Arizona. Their culture lasted from about 100BCE until Spanish missionaries, soldiers and settlers arrived at the end of the sixteenth century. 'mesa': table-land.

p. 235 'The Roses of Camon': Camon is a small village in Aude, France, celebrated for its many varieties of roses. The verses in French are by Pierre de Ronsard (1524-1585).

p. 242 'What She Promises': the book in question is Shusha Guppy's *The Secret of Laughter: Magical Tales from Classical Persia*.

p. 246 'The Syrian Goddess': Atargatis, widely known as the 'Syrian Goddess', was Great Mother of earth and water. She was depicted as a mermaid.

p. 254 'Sea-Dew': the name Rosemary derives from the Latin *hros maris*, dew of the sea.

p. 257 'Seahenge: A Journey': Seahenge was a timber circle. It consisted of 55 split oak trunks and at its centre was a huge oak stump, upside down. It was constructed in 2049 BCE and discovered, standing on the foreshore near Holme in Norfolk, in 1999. In poems 3-6, a young woman tells how she helped to build the circle and lay the body of her father within it.

p. 264 'Time's Fool': written in response to Shakespeare's Sonnet 60, 'Like as the waves make towards the pebbled shore.'

p. 269 'Your Sea-Voice': quotations from *Archipelago 12* (Summer, 2019) and *Sailing to an Island* (Faber, 1963).

p. 272 'L'Abbaye-Château de Camon': the medieval fortified house and Abbey adjoin one another.
Aliénor: Eleanor of Acquitaine.
Félicien: patron saint of the Abbey.

p. 280 'As It Is': the poem is set in the North Cascades.

p. 281 'Tug-of-War': for many years there has been an annual summer tug-of-war across the River Thame between the villages of Ickford in Buckinghamshire and Tiddington in Oxfordshire.

p. 295 'In a Norfolk Garden': italicised quotations by William Shakespeare; anonymous; Will Kemp; Peter Scupham; George Crabbe; Anthony Thwaite.

p. 323 'Moth-Light: 1959': Mary Ann was the youngest surviving child of Robert Evans, a land agent in Warwickshire. She took the name of George Eliot when she began to publish stories.

ALPHABETIC LIST OF POEMS

BIOGRAPHICAL NOTE

KEVIN CROSSLEY-HOLLAND is a prize-winning poet, children's author, translator, librettist, and editor. He won the Carnegie Medal and the Guardian Children's Fiction prize, and his *Arthur* trilogy was translated into twenty-six languages. He is the author of *The Penguin Book of Norse Myths, Arthur the Always King*, and celebrated retellings of British folktales, and has translated *Beowulf* and many of the shorter Old English poems.

His memoir of childhood, *The Hidden Roads*, revolving around the sanctity and splintering of family, is steeped in the landscape and layers of England, and was highly praised by Rowan Williams, while Philip Pullman has written of his work, "Kevin Crossley-Holland is a master, a magician and commander of the language, the roots of whose work are deeply entwined with ancient patterns of truth and knowledge. I salute and venerate him."

Kevin was poetry editor for Macmillan and then editorial director for Victor Gollancz. In this capacity, he built poetry lists that included R. S. Thomas, Elizabeth Jennings, Charles Causley, Michael Longley, Geoffrey Grigson, Eavan Boland, Peter Dale, Iain Crichton Smith, Ruth Fainlight, Alan Brownjohn, and many another. He has collaborated with many leading composers, including Sir Arthur Bliss, Nicola LeFanu, Bob Chilcott, Bernard Hughes and Cecilia McDowall, and artists including Charles Keeping, John Lawrence, Norman Ackroyd, Chris Riddell and Andrew Rafferty.

He is a Fellow of the Royal Society of Literature and the Society of Authors, and an Honorary Fellow of Saint Edmund Hall, Oxford. His archive is housed in the Brotherton Collection at Leeds University. He has a Minnesotan wife, four children and nine grandchildren, and lives in North Norfolk.